r i c e & noodle

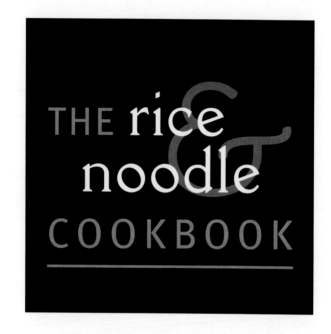

# THE rice & noodle COOKBOOK

## 100 delicious step-by-step recipes

Consultant editors:
Christine Ingram and Roz Denny

LORENZ BOOKS

First published in 1999 by Lorenz Books

© Anness Publishing Limited 1999

Lorenz Books is an imprint of
Anness Publishing Limited
Hermes House
88–89 Blackfriars Road
London SE1 8HA

This edition distributed in Canada by Raincoast Books
8680 Cambie Street
Vancouver
British Columbia, V6P 6M9

ISBN 1 85967 906 4

A CIP catalogue record for this book is available from the British Library

**Publisher:** Joanna Lorenz
**Senior Cookery Editor:** Linda Fraser
**Project Editors:** Zoe Antoniou, Margaret Malone and Emma Clegg
**Designers:** Joyce Chester and Lilian Lindblom
**Jacket Designer:** Luise Roberts
**Photographers:** Karl Adamson, Edward Allwright, David Armstrong, Steve Baxter,
James Duncan, Michelle Garrett, Amanda Heywood, Tim Hill, Janine Hosegood,
David Jordan, Don Last, William Lingwood, Patrick McLeavey, Michael Michaels,
Thomas Odulate and Juliet Piddington.
**Recipes:** Alex Barker, Carla Capalbo, Kit Chan, Frances Cleary,
Roz Denny, Matthew Drennan, Sarah Edmonds, Rafi Fernandez, Christine France,
Silvana Franco, Sarah Gates, Shirley Gill, Rosamund Grant, Janine Hosegood, Deh-
Ta Hsiung, Shehzad Husain, Peter Jordan, Manisha Kanani, Soheila Kimberley,
Masaki Ko, Ruby Le Bois, Patricia Lousada, Lesley Mackley, Norma MacMillan, Sue
Maggs, Sarah Maxwell, Sallie Morris, Janice Murfitt, Angela Nilsen, Elisabeth
Lambert Ortiz, Maggie Pannell, Anne Sheasby, Liz Trigg, Hilaire Walden,
Laura Washburn, Steven Wheeler and Elizabeth Wolf-Cohen.
**Stylists:** Madeleine Brehaut, Clare Hunt, Maria Kelly, Marion McLornan,
Blake Minton, Marion Price and Elizabeth Wolf-Cohen.
**Food for photography:** Jacqueline Clark, Joanne Craig, Katherine Hawkins,
Jane Stevenson, Carol Tennant and Judy Williams.

Previously published as two separate titles:
*50 Delicious Noodle Dishes* and *50 Classic Rice Recipes*

Printed and bound in Hong Kong/China

1 2 3 4 5 6 7 8 9 10

# contents

## rice 6

## noodles 98

# rice

long grain

basmati rice

brown rice

red rice

Wehani rice

Thai rice

white rice

wild rice

short grain

glutinous rice

pudding rice

risotto rice

carnaroli rice

arborio rice

Vialone Nano

# INTRODUCING RICE

Rice is central to many of the world's greatest cuisines and can be used in a host of ways, both savoury and sweet. No other food is quite this versatile. In the West, we have just begun to appreciate the great potential of this glorious grain and instead of relegating it to the side of our plates as an accompaniment, we now look upon rice as the basis of a delicious meal.

Around two-thirds of the world's population are nourished every day on rice. There are thought to be about 7,000 varieties of rice grown across the globe, all with different qualities and characteristics. The term "rice" should be applied to the milled grain only, while the actual plant is known as paddy. Rice is highly recommended by doctors and nutritionists as it is high in carbohydrates and low in fat, making it a healthy form of energy that is also easily digestible.

Rice was one of the first cereals to be cultivated thousands of years ago from a variety of wild grasses in many different parts of Asia. There was no one specific birthplace. The numerous varieties common today in rice-eating countries evolved according to the climate and terrain and the developing agricultural practices of the time. Even today, many new strains of rice continue to be developed.

The main rice-growing regions of the world are China, Japan, India, Indonesia, Thailand, the southern states of the USA and areas of Spain and Italy. The great joy of rice cooking is the incredible variety of dishes one can make. There are the shaped sushi of Japan, the pressed rice cakes of Thailand, pilaus of India, pilaffs of the Middle East, risottos and paellas of the Mediterranean, jambalayas of America and rice 'n' peas of the West Indies – the list can be endless and the variety inspirational.

# Types of Rice

Rice is selected for a dish according to the length of the grain. There are two main categories for rice, long and short grain.

## Long Grain Rices

Long grain rices (*oryza indica*) contain high levels of amylase starch, which keeps the grains more separate after cooking. They are excellent steamed or baked, in pilaus and salads. Long grain rices are also known collectively as Patna rices because much of the long grain rice sold to Europe originally came from around Patna in India.

### Basmati Rice

This long grain rice is highly aromatic and its name means "fragrant" in Hindi. It is ideal for delicate pilaus. Basmati rice benefits from rinsing in a bowl with plenty of cold water and a soaking for 30 minutes before cooking to lighten the grain.

### Brown Rice

This long grain rice has its husk removed, leaving a nutritious bran layer. It is therefore higher in fibre and has a slightly nutty taste and chewy texture. This rice can take up to 40 minutes to cook, so more water will be required to allow for this longer cooking time. Brown (and white) long grain rice is available in par-boiled or easy-cook versions, which means that it has been heat treated with high pressure steam, making it non-stick. This does, however, remove much of the natural flavour and the rice can take longer to cook and has an even chewier texture. Brown basmati is lighter than other brown grains and it takes about 25 minutes to cook.

### Red Rices

In the wild, rice is actually a light red colour. Sometimes this characteristic is bred back into long grain rices. Examples of these rices are the Wehani rice from California and more recently a semi-wild cultivated red rice from the Camargue, France, similar to buckwheat in flavour.

### Thai Rices

Thai fragrant or Thai jasmine are high quality long grain rices that have a slight stickiness to them and a delicate fragrance. They take even less time to cook than basmati and are best cooked by the covered pan/absorption method with one-and-a-quarter-times the volume of water to rice. No salt is added during cooking.

### White Rice

This is the most widely used long grain rice and is mild in flavour. Most long grain rice sold in Europe originates from America and is of excellent quality, especially rice that is grown in Arkansas, Texas and California.

### Wild Rice

This is not actually a true rice at all but a form of aquatic grass found growing around lakes in Canada and North America. The best type of wild rice is long, dark brown and glossy. The grains should be cooked until they burst open so releasing their natural deliciously nutty aroma. They take up to 50 minutes to cook, and need to be well submerged in water for most of that time. A form of smaller grain, cultivated wild rice is more readily available and cheaper. It can sometimes also be found in a blend with easy-cook long grains.

## Short Grain Rices

Short grain rice (*oryza japonica*), or round grain, is high in amylopectin, which gives a starchy quality so that the grains cling together after cooking.

### Glutinous Rices

These are more sticky than Thai rices. The name is misleading as the grains contain no gluten. These rices are also ideal for sushi as the rice sticks together for shaping and rolling. Japanese rice is a short grain glutinous rice, easy for picking up and dipping into sauces. Glutinous rices can be black or white and are often used for puddings.

### Pudding Rice

Short grain rice is often packaged as pudding rice because the grains absorb much liquid to make a creamy, rich texture that is essential for milk puddings. Short grain rice can be used for risotto, croquettes, sushi and some stir-fried dishes.

### Risotto Rices

These short grain rices have high levels of starch. Good risotto rice gives a nice creaminess to a dish yet the grain still retains an *al dente* bite. Some of the best risotto rices are carnaroli, arborio and Vialone Nano. Stock is added gradually when making risotto, but if making paella with this grain, add the stock all at once and simmer without stirring.

*Left (clockwise from top left): arborio and three varieties of carnaroli rices.*
*Right: brown, long grain, easy-cook, brown basmati, basmati and American long grain rices (centre).*

# Equipment

The list of equipment that is useful in a kitchen is endless. Some utensils are particularly handy when preparing rice, and will make cooking your favourite dishes so much easier.

### Colander
This is essential for draining the water from rice when it has been rinsed or boiled. Use a colander with small holes.

### Food Processor
The food processor is useful for mixing and blending ingredients. Most have an attachment for slicing and grating large quantities, which helps to prepare ingredients more quickly, especially since some rice does not take a long time to cook.

### Fork
Use a fork to simply fluff up the grains of cooked rice.

### Frying Pan
This is useful for sautéed rice. Frying pans are also useful if you are preparing stir-fry recipes when a wok is unavailable.

### Hand Whisk
A sturdy hand whisk is useful for beating eggs, combining ingredients such as salad dressings and for mixing sauces to a smooth consistency. The best ones are made of stainless steel.

### Measuring Cups and Spoons
Measuring cups and spoons are useful for gauging accurately the volume and corresponding weight of ingredients. Spoon measures range from 2.5 ml/½ tsp to 15 ml/1 tbsp and cups from 50 ml/2 fl oz/¼ cup to 250 ml/ 8 fl oz/1 cup.

### Mixing Bowls
Glass mixing bowls that fit neatly inside each other are useful for a number of recipe preparations such as making rice salads or mixing desserts.

### Pestle and Mortar
This is useful for grinding small amounts of spices, and it is worth buying one if you enjoy cooking with fresh spices regularly.

### Rice Cooker
Rice cookers are very useful and make a good investment if you cook rice regularly. They can produce good results with rice, and will free the stove for cooking other ingredients. They are more suitable for cooking sticky and easy-cook grains than basmati rice, which needs to be par-boiled first. A rice cooker will also keep rice warm for up to five hours. Leftover rice can be reheated the following day and the cooker can also be used for steaming many other dishes.

### Rice Paddle
This is an ideal utensil for serving cooked rice.

### Saucepan
A good stainless-steel saucepan with a tight-fitting lid is essential for cooking rice properly. It is a sound investment for any cook. The best pans tend to be sold individually rather than as a set. They are expensive but will last a lifetime of simmering and boiling.

### Steamers
Steamers are used for cooking sticky rice or sticky rice balls. Where these small items are being cooked, line the baskets with pieces of rinsed muslin. Bamboo, stacking-type steamers are available in many sizes from a wide range of stores. When not in use, they look very attractive on a shelf in the kitchen. Like almost all utensils in the oriental kitchen, they are multi-purpose. Indeed the baskets can be used for serving as well as cooking the foods.

### Wok
The wok is ideal for stir-frying a number of rice dishes. There are several varieties available including the carbon steel round-bottomed wok or Pau wok. This is best suited to a gas hob, where you will be able to control the amount of heat needed more easily. The carbon steel flat-bottomed wok is best for use on electric or solid fuel hobs, as it will give a better distribution of heat. One useful cooking tip is to warm the wok gently before adding the oil for cooking. The oil then floods easily over the surface of the warm pan and prevents the food from sticking. Less oil is required when using a wok than in conventional pans. Always heat a wok before adding cooking oil.

*Right: a selection of some of the most common and useful kitchen utensils.*

# Plain Long Grain Rice

Use white long grain rice throughout, unless otherwise specified, and remember to adjust your cooking method if using a different grain.

### The Open Pan/Fast Boiling Method

This is the simplest method. The rice is cooked in a large amount of boiling water over a medium heat until *al dente*. It is then drained and rinsed. Long grain white rice will take about 15 minutes to cook, and brown rice 30–35 minutes. If using easy-cook rice, follow the directions on the packet.

### The Covered Pan/Absorption Method

For this method (shown here) the rice is steamed. The rice simmers gently in a measured amount of water in a covered saucepan until all the water has been absorbed. This has the added bonus of retaining valuable nutrients that would be discarded in the water if the rice were boiled.

*Serves 4*

INGREDIENTS
250 g/9 oz/1⅓ cups white long grain rice
pinch of salt

## COOK'S TIP

Precisely how much liquid to use, and the cooking time, will vary depending on the type of rice used, the width of the saucepan (and how snugly its lid fits) and the heat of the hob. For 250 g/9 oz/1⅓ cups brown rice, use 600 ml/1 pint/2½ cups water and cook for 25–35 minutes.

**1** Wash the rice in several changes of cold water to remove excess starch, and drain. This is important as the rice is not rinsed at the end, as it is with the boiling method. Place the rice in a saucepan and add 475 ml/16 fl oz/2 cups cold water. (There should be no more than about 1.5 cm/⅔ in of water above the surface of the rice.)

**2** Bring to the boil and add the salt, then stir to prevent the rice sticking to the bottom of the pan. Reduce the heat to very, very low, cover the pan tightly and cook for 15–20 minutes, or until all the water has been absorbed.

**3** Remove from the heat and leave to stand with the lid on for 5–10 minutes. Fluff up the rice with a fork or spoon just before serving. Rice cooked by the boiling method should also be fluffed up before being served.

## VARIATIONS

There are a number of other ways to cook rice. These are more commonly used when rice is cooked with other ingredients in a recipe, such as a stir-fry or bake. Follow the instructions below to sauté or bake rice. See the Covered Pan/Absorption Method (opposite) for quantities and timings but use boiling rather than cold water. You may need more water when cooking by the sauté method.

**1** ▲To sauté rice, heat a small amount of oil, butter, or a mixture of the two in a saucepan over a medium heat. Add the rice and stir to coat the grains. Sauté for 2–3 minutes, stirring constantly.

**2** Add the measured quantity of boiling salted water. Bring back to the boil, then cover and steam over a very low heat until all the water has been absorbed and the rice is tender.

**1** ▲To bake rice, preheat the oven to 180°C/350°F/Gas 4. Place the washed and rinsed rice in a baking dish and add the measured boiling salted water.

**2** Cover tightly with foil or a lid and bake until the water has been absorbed and the rice is tender; 20–30 minutes for white rice and 35–40 for brown. Cooking time depends on many factors, including how tightly covered the dish is.

## REHEATING RICE

Always reheat cooked rice thoroughly for at least 5 minutes until it is piping hot, especially if stir-frying. This is very important, as cooked rice can harbour spores of bacteria. If rice is reheated on several occasions, or kept warm for a long time, the bacteria may germinate and multiply. Food poisoning could result.

## STORING RICE

Cooked leftover rice can be stored for up to 2 days in the fridge. Rice can be frozen, but this affects the starch granules, making them seem chalky when reheated.

# Rice for Salads

This recipe uses cooked rice. Try to cook rice freshly for a salad rather than use leftover cold rice, as the result is much nicer. This is a basic recipe for a rice salad but you can add a variety of ingredients.

### Serves 4

INGREDIENTS
175 g/6 oz/scant 1 cup long grain rice, cooked
75 ml/5 tbsp selected vinaigrette
75 g/3 oz/¹/₂ cup black olives
40 g/1¹/₂ oz/¹/₂ cup chopped spring onions
50 g/2 oz/¹/₂ cup chopped celery
75 g/3 oz/¹/₂ cup chopped radishes
50 g/2 oz/¹/₂ cup chopped cucumber
salt and freshly ground black pepper
parsley sprigs, to garnish

**1** Place the cooked, rinsed and drained rice in a bowl and add the vinaigrette of your choice, together with seasoning. Allow the mixture to stand for a good 15 minutes. This method ensures a delicious, light salad where the dressing has been absorbed right into the grain instead of a more cloying dressing that simply coats the side.

**2** Quarter the olives, discarding the stones, and add to the rice with the other ingredients. Toss well and garnish with sprigs of parsley.

# Basmati Rice

In India, basmati rice is consumed in great quantities by all members of society. Using ghee instead of butter or oil creates an authentic flavour.

*Serves 4*

INGREDIENTS
4 ml/³/₄ tsp ghee, unsalted butter or olive oil
250 g/9 oz/1¹/₃ cups basmati rice, washed and drained
salt, to taste

**1** Heat the ghee, butter or oil in a saucepan and sauté the drained rice thoroughly for about 2–3 minutes.

**2** Add 475 ml/16 fl oz/2 cups of water and salt and bring to the boil. Reduce the heat to low, cover and cook gently for 15–20 minutes until all the water is absorbed. Stand, covered, for 5 minutes. Fluff the grains before serving.

# Jasmine Rice

A naturally aromatic, long grain white rice, jasmine rice is the staple of most Thai meals. Salt is not added to this delicate rice during cooking.

*Serves 4*

INGREDIENTS
350 g/12 oz/1³/₄ cups jasmine rice

**1** Rinse the rice thoroughly in cold water, until the water runs clear. Place the rice in a heavy-based saucepan and add 600 ml/1 pint/2¹/₂ cups cold water. Bring the rice to a vigorous boil, uncovered, over a high heat.

**2** Stir and reduce the heat to low. Cover and simmer for 12–15 minutes, or until all the water has been absorbed. Remove from the heat and leave to stand for 10 minutes. Fluff up and separate the grains with a fork.

# Wild Rice

This aquatic grass is deliciously nutty and firm. It is cooked in the same way as long grain rice, but needs a longer cooking time.

*Serves 4*

INGREDIENTS
pinch of salt
250 g/9 oz/generous 1 cup wild rice

**I** Place 1 litre/1¾ pints/4 cups cold water in a saucepan and add the salt. Bring to the boil.

**2** ▲ Add the rice to the saucepan and bring back to the boil. Cook the rice for about 45–50 minutes. The rice is ready when it has become tender but still firm and the grains have begun to split open. Drain well and serve.

## COOK'S TIP
Wild rice perfectly complements meat and poultry dishes. It is also an excellent partner for vegetables such as winter squashes and mushrooms.

# Glutinous Rice

The term glutinous is a little misleading as the rice does not actually contain gluten. It is also known as sticky rice and can be black as well as white.

*Serves 4*

INGREDIENTS
450 g/1 lb/2⅔ cups glutinous (sticky) rice
5 ml/1 tsp vegetable oil
2.5 ml/½ tsp salt

**I** Rinse the rice in cold water until it runs clear. Place in a bowl with plenty of water and leave to soak for 1 hour.

**2** ▲ Drain, tip into a bowl and add the oil and salt. Line a large steamer with a piece of clean muslin or cheesecloth. Transfer the rice to this. Steam over boiling water for about 45 minutes, stirring from time to time.

## COOK'S TIP
Glutinous rice is often served as a pudding, particularly in Thailand. It can be accompanied simply with sugar and coconut cream.

# Risotto Rice

This short grain rice absorbs cooking liquid and becomes beautifully creamy. A risotto can be served as a first course, a main dish or an accompaniment. This recipe is basic but flavoursome. The garlic can be omitted.

## Serves 4

INGREDIENTS

1.3 litres/2¼ pints/5½ cups chicken stock
25 g/1 oz/2 tbsp butter or oil
½ onion, chopped
2 garlic cloves, crushed (optional)
350 g/12 oz/1¾ cups risotto rice

risotto rice

oil

garlic

onion

chicken stock

**1** In a saucepan, bring the stock to the boil, then reduce the heat so that the liquid is kept at a gentle simmer.

**2** Heat the butter or oil, or a mixture of the two, in a wide, heavy saucepan. Add the chopped onion and crushed garlic, if using, and cook over a low heat until soft, stirring occasionally.

## COOK'S TIP

You can use arborio rice for risottos throughout, if you like, as it is a good medium grain risotto rice, while superfine arborio rice is one of the best. This swells to at least three times its original size during cooking, which enables the rice to absorb all the cooking liquid for a creamy, smooth texture while still retaining the shape of the grains.

**3** Add the rice and stir to coat it with the fat. Sauté for 1–2 minutes over a moderate heat, stirring.

**4** Add a little of the simmering stock (about a ladleful) and stir well. Simmer, stirring frequently, until the rice has absorbed almost all the liquid.

**5** Add a little more of the simmering stock and cook, stirring, until it is almost all absorbed. Continue adding the stock in this way until the grains of rice are tender but still firm to the bite, or *al dente*, and the risotto is creamy but not runny. You may not need to add all the stock. Total cooking time will be about 30 minutes.

# Japanese Rice for Sushi

The Japanese prefer their rice slightly sticky so that it can be easily eaten with chopsticks, shaped into rice balls or used to make sushi. Use Japanese rice if you can find it, otherwise substitute Thai or long grain rice.

*Serves 4*

INGREDIENTS
350 g/12 oz/1¾ cups Japanese rice, washed and drained
1 piece giant kelp, 5 cm/2 in square (optional)

MIXED VINEGAR
45 ml/3 tbsp rice vinegar or distilled white vinegar
45 ml/3 tbsp granulated sugar
10 ml/2 tsp sea salt

kelp

Japanese
rice

salt

sugar

rice
vinegar

**1** Place the rice in a large heavy saucepan, cover with 1.2 litres/2 pints/5 cups boiling water and add the kelp, if using. Stir once and simmer, uncovered, for 15 minutes. Turn off the heat, cover and stand for a further 5 minutes to allow the rice to finish cooking in its own steam. Before serving, the rice should be fluffed with chopsticks or a fork. This rice is a Japanese staple.

## COOK'S TIP

The washing process for Japanese rice is very important as it improves the flavour of the cooked rice. It must be washed several times in cold water until the water runs clear. Thai or long grain rice should only be washed once for sushi recipes, so that the grains become slightly sticky when cooked. Note that cooked Japanese rice should not be stored in the fridge as it will go hard.

**2** To prepare sushi rice, make the dressing by heating the vinegar in a small saucepan, with a lid to keep in the strong vapours. Add the sugar and salt and dissolve. Allow to cool. Spread the cooked rice on to a mat or tray and allow to cool.

**3** Pour on the dressing and fluff with chopsticks or a fork. Keep covered until ready to use.

# Beef and Rice Soup

This classic Iranian soup, *Aashe Maste*, is extremely substantial and almost makes a meal in itself. It is full of invigorating herbs, and is a popular cold weather dish.

*Serves 6*

INGREDIENTS
2 large onions
30 ml/2 tbsp oil
15 ml/1 tbsp ground turmeric
90 g/3½ oz/½ cup yellow split peas
225 g/8 oz minced beef
200 g/7 oz/1 cup long grain rice
45 ml/3 tbsp each chopped fresh
    parsley, coriander and chives
2–3 saffron strands
15 g/½ oz/1 tbsp butter
1 large garlic clove, finely chopped
60 ml/4 tbsp chopped fresh mint
salt and freshly ground black pepper
yogurt and naan bread, to serve

*onions*        *oil*

*yellow split peas*     *minced beef*     *garlic*     *ground turmeric*     *saffron*     *parsley*

*chives*

*long grain rice*     *yogurt*

*mint*     *coriander*     *butter*

**1** Chop one of the onions then heat the oil in a large saucepan and fry the onion until golden brown. Add the turmeric, split peas and 1.2 litres/2 pints/5 cups water, bring to the boil, then reduce the heat and simmer for about 20 minutes.

**2** Grate the other onion into a bowl, add the minced beef and seasoning and mix well. Using your hands, form the mixture into small balls, about the size of walnuts. Carefully add to the pan and simmer for 10 minutes.

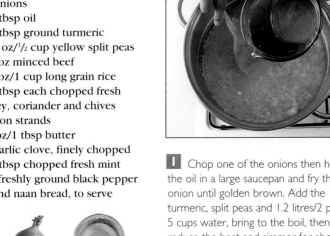

**3** Add the rice, then stir in the parsley, coriander, and chives and simmer for about 30 minutes, until the rice is tender, stirring frequently. Infuse the saffron in 15 ml/1 tbsp boiling water.

**4** Melt the butter in a small pan and gently fry the garlic. Add the mint, stir briefly and sprinkle over the soup with the saffron and its liquid. Spoon the soup into warmed serving dishes and serve with yogurt and naan bread.

## COOK'S TIP
Fresh spinach is also delicious in this soup. Add 50 g/2 oz finely chopped spinach leaves to the soup with the parsley, coriander and chives.

# Stuffed Vine Leaves

Based on the Greek dolmades, but with a vegetarian brown rice stuffing, this makes an excellent starter, snack or buffet dish.

## Makes about 40

INGREDIENTS

15 ml/1 tbsp sunflower oil
5 ml/1 tsp sesame oil
1 onion, finely chopped
225 g/8 oz/1¼ cups brown rice
600 ml/1 pint/2½ cups vegetable stock
1 small yellow pepper, seeded and finely chopped
115 g/4 oz/½ cup ready-to-eat dried apricots, finely chopped
2 lemons
50 g/2 oz/⅔ cup pine nuts
45 ml/3 tbsp chopped fresh parsley
30 ml/2 tbsp chopped fresh mint
2.5 ml/½ tsp mixed spice
225 g/8 oz packet vine leaves preserved in brine, drained
30 ml/2 tbsp olive oil
freshly ground black pepper
lemon wedges, to garnish

TO SERVE

300 ml/½ pint/1¼ cups low-fat natural yogurt
30 ml/2 tbsp chopped mixed fresh herbs
cayenne pepper

yogurt

cayenne pepper

mint

mixed herbs

pine nuts

sunflower oil

sesame oil

onion

yellow pepper

parsley

olive oil

vine leaves

mixed spice

brown rice

vegetable stock

dried apricots

lemons

**1** Heat the sunflower and sesame oils together in a large saucepan. Add the onion and cook gently for 5 minutes to soften. Add the rice, stirring to coat the grains in oil. Pour in the stock, bring to the boil, then lower the heat, cover the pan and simmer for 30 minutes, or until the rice is tender but *al dente*.

**2** Stir in the chopped pepper and apricots, with a little more stock if necessary. Replace the lid and cook for a further 5 minutes. Grate the rind from one of the lemons then squeeze both.

**3** Drain off any stock which has not been absorbed by the rice. Stir in the pine nuts, herbs, mixed spice, grated lemon rind and half the juice. Season with pepper and set aside.

**5** Pack the parcels closely together in a shallow serving dish. Mix the remaining lemon juice with the olive oil. Pour the mixture over the vine leaves, cover and chill before serving. Garnish with lemon wedges. Spoon the yogurt into a bowl, stir in the chopped herbs and sprinkle with a little cayenne. Serve with the stuffed vine leaves.

**4** Bring a saucepan of water to the boil and blanch the vine leaves for 5 minutes. Drain the leaves well, then lay them shiny side down on a board. Cut out any coarse stalks. Place a heap of the rice mixture in the centre of each vine leaf. Fold the stem end over, then the sides and pointed end to make neat parcels.

## COOK'S TIP

If vine leaves are not available, the leaves of Swiss chard, young spinach or cabbage can be used instead.

# Thai Rice Cakes with Spicy Dipping Sauce

Start cooking this recipe the day before you want to serve it, as it involves some lengthy preparation.

## Serves 4-6

INGREDIENTS
175 g/6 oz/scant 1 cup jasmine rice
oil for deep-fat frying and greasing

FOR THE SPICY DIPPING SAUCE
6-8 dried chillies
2.5 ml/½ tsp salt
2 shallots, chopped
2 garlic cloves, chopped
4 coriander roots
10 white peppercorns
250 ml/8 fl oz/1 cup coconut milk
5 ml/1 tsp shrimp paste
115 g/4 oz minced pork
115 g/4 oz cherry tomatoes, chopped
15 ml/1 tbsp fish sauce
15 ml/1 tbsp palm sugar
30 ml/2 tbsp tamarind juice
30 ml/2 tbsp coarsely chopped
    roasted peanuts
2 spring onions, finely chopped
mint sprigs, to garnish

oil

dried chillies

shallots

shrimp paste

spring onions

roasted peanuts

garlic

cherry tomatoes

jasmine rice

coriander roots

coconut milk

white peppercorns

minced pork

fish sauce

tamarind juice

**1** Make the sauce. Cut along the stem of each chilli and remove most of the seeds. Soak the chillies in warm water for 20 minutes. Drain and transfer to a mortar. Add the salt and grind with a pestle until crushed. Add the shallots, garlic, coriander roots and peppercorns. Pound to make a coarse paste.

**2** Pour the coconut milk into a saucepan and boil until it begins to separate. Add the chilli paste. Cook for 2–3 minutes, stir in the shrimp paste and cook for 1 minute. Add the pork and cook for 5–10 minutes, stirring well.

**3** Add the tomatoes, fish sauce, palm sugar and tamarind juice. Simmer until the sauce thickens. Stir in the chopped peanuts and spring onions. Remove from the heat and leave to cool. Chill the mixture overnight.

**4** Wash the rice. Place in a saucepan, add 300 ml/½ pint/1¼ cups water and cover. Bring to the boil, reduce the heat and simmer for 12–15 minutes. Remove the lid and fluff up the rice. Turn out on to a lightly greased tray and press down. Leave to dry out overnight in a very low oven until dry and firm.

**5** Remove the rice from the tray and break into bite-size pieces. Heat the oil in a wok or deep-fat fryer. Deep fry the rice cakes in batches for about 1 minute, until they puff up, taking care not to brown them too much. Remove and drain. Garnish with mint sprigs and serve with the spicy dipping sauce.

# Sticky Rice Balls Filled with Chicken

These balls can either be steamed or deep fried. The fried versions are crunchy and are excellent for serving at drinks parties.

*Makes about 30*

INGREDIENTS
450 g/1 lb minced chicken
1 egg
15 ml/1 tbsp tapioca flour
4 spring onions, finely chopped
30 ml/2 tbsp chopped fresh
    coriander
30 ml/2 tbsp fish sauce
pinch of sugar
75 g/3 oz/⅓ cup glutinous (sticky)
    rice, cooked
banana leaves
oil for brushing
freshly ground black pepper
sweet chilli sauce, to serve

FOR THE GARNISH
1 small carrot, shredded
1 red pepper, cut into strips
snipped chives

*spring onions*

*glutinous rice*

*tapioca flour*

*minced chicken*

*egg*

*sugar*

*coriander*

*banana leaves*

*fish sauce*

*carrot*

*chives*

*sweet chilli sauce*

*red pepper*

## COOK'S TIP
Try to find banana leaves for this recipe as they impart their own subtle flavour of fine tea. The leaves are used in Thai cooking for wrapping foods as well as lining steamers.

**1** In a mixing bowl, combine the minced chicken, egg, tapioca flour, spring onions and coriander. Mix well and season with fish sauce, sugar and freshly ground black pepper.

**2** Using chopsticks, spread the cooked sticky rice on a plate or flat tray.

**3** Place teaspoonfuls of some of the chicken mixture on the bed of rice, placing them evenly spaced apart. With damp hands, roll and shape this mixture in the rice to make a ball about the size of a walnut. Repeat with the rest of the chicken mixture.

**4** Line a bamboo steamer with banana leaves and lightly brush them with oil. Place the chicken balls on the leaves, spacing well apart to prevent them from sticking together. Steam over a high heat for about 10 minutes or until cooked. Remove and arrange on serving plates. Garnish with shredded carrot, red pepper and chives. Serve with sweet chilli sauce as a dip.

# Rice Balls Filled with Manchego Cheese

For a really impressive Spanish tapa-style snack, serve these delicious rice balls.

## Serves 6

INGREDIENTS
1 globe artichoke
50 g/2 oz/¼ cup butter
1 small onion, finely chopped
1 garlic clove, finely chopped
115 g/4 oz/⅔ cup risotto rice
450 ml/¾ pint/scant 2 cups hot
    chicken stock
50 g/2 oz/⅔ cup freshly grated
    Parmesan cheese
150 g/5 oz Manchego cheese, very
    finely diced
45–60 ml/3–4 tbsp polenta
olive oil for frying
salt and freshly ground black pepper
flat leaf parsley, to garnish

artichoke

onion

butter

polenta

risotto rice

chicken stock

garlic

Parmesan cheese

olive oil

Manchego cheese

flat leaf parsley

**1** Remove the stalk, leaves and choke to leave just the heart of the artichoke. Chop the heart finely.

**2** Melt the butter in a saucepan and gently fry the chopped artichoke heart, onion and garlic for 5 minutes until softened. Stir in the rice and cook for about 1 minute.

## COOK'S TIP
Manchego cheese is made with sheep's milk from La Mancha in Spain. It is ideal for grating or grilling.

**3** Keeping the heat fairly high, gradually add the stock, stirring constantly until all the liquid has been absorbed and the rice is cooked – this should take about 20 minutes. Season well, then stir in the Parmesan. Transfer to a bowl. Leave to cool, then cover and chill for at least 2 hours.

**4** Spoon about 15 ml/1 tbsp of the mixture into one hand, flatten slightly, and place a few pieces of diced Manchego cheese in the centre. Shape to make a small ball. Flatten, then lightly roll in the polenta. Make about 12 cakes in total. Shallow fry in hot olive oil for about 4–5 minutes until the rice cakes are crisp and golden brown. Drain on kitchen paper and serve hot, garnished with parsley.

# Rice Omelette

Rice is an unusual omelette filling in the West, but Japanese children love this recipe, and often top the omelettes with tomato ketchup.

### Serves 4

INGREDIENTS

115 g/4 oz skinless, boneless chicken thighs, cut into 1 cm/½ in cubes
35 ml/7 tsp butter
1 small onion, chopped
1 carrot, chopped
2 shiitake or closed cup mushrooms, stems removed, caps chopped
15 ml/1 tbsp finely chopped fresh parsley
150 g/5 oz/¾ cup Japanese rice, cooked
30 ml/2 tbsp tomato ketchup
6 large eggs
60 ml/4 tbsp milk
salt and freshly ground black or white pepper
fresh parsley sprigs, to garnish
tomato ketchup, to serve (optional)

*chicken thighs*  *onion*  *butter*  *carrot*  *mushrooms*  *milk*  *Japanese rice*  *tomato ketchup*  *parsley*  *eggs*

## COOK'S TIP

Shiitake mushrooms are the most popular ones in Japan. They have a good flavour, especially when dried. If they are dried, soak them in a bowl of cold water for 20 minutes, placing a small saucer on top to keep the mushrooms submerged. Drain, but keep the soaking water if you like, as it makes a good stock.

**1** Season the chicken with salt and pepper. Melt 7.5 ml/1½ tsp butter in a frying pan. Fry the onion for 1 minute, then add the chicken and fry until the chicken is white and cooked. Add the carrots and mushrooms, stir-fry until soft over a moderate heat, then add the parsley. Set this mixture aside and wipe the frying pan clean.

**2** Melt 7.5 ml/1½ tsp butter in the frying pan, add the rice and stir well. Mix in the fried ingredients, tomato ketchup and pepper. Stir well, adding salt to taste if necessary. Keep the mixture warm. Beat the eggs lightly, add the milk, 2.5 ml/½ tsp salt and pepper.

**3** Melt 5 ml/1 tsp butter in an omelette pan over a moderate heat. Pour in a quarter of the egg mixture and stir it briefly with a fork, then leave to set for 1 minute. Top with a quarter of the rice mixture.

**4** Fold the omelette over the rice and slide it to the edge of the pan to shape it into a curve. Do not cook the omelette too much. Invert the omelette on to a warmed plate, cover with kitchen paper and press neatly into a rectangular shape. Cook another three omelettes from the remaining ingredients. Serve immediately with tomato ketchup drizzled on top, if you like. Garnish with parsley.

# Rice Croquettes

These delicious croquettes are actually made from paella and are served as a tapa, a snack or a starter, in Spain. The paella is cooked from scratch here, but you can use leftover paella instead.

## Serves 4

INGREDIENTS
pinch of saffron strands
150 ml/¼ pint/⅔ cup white wine
30 ml/2 tbsp olive oil
1 small onion, finely chopped
1 garlic clove, finely chopped
115 g/4 oz/⅔ cup risotto rice
300 ml/½ pint/1¼ cups hot chicken stock
50 g/2 oz cooked prawns, peeled, deveined and roughly chopped
50 g/2 oz cooked chicken, roughly chopped
50 g/2 oz/½ cup petits pois, thawed if frozen
30 ml/2 tbsp freshly grated Parmesan cheese
1 egg, beaten
30 ml/2 tbsp milk
75 g/3 oz/1½ cups fresh white breadcrumbs
vegetable or olive oil, for frying
salt and freshly ground black pepper
fresh flat leaf parsley, to garnish

*saffron*

*white wine*

*olive oil*

*garlic*

*onion*

*egg*

*parsley*

*risotto rice*

*chicken stock*

*Parmesan cheese*

*oil*

*prawns*

*cooked chicken*

*petits pois*

*milk*

*breadcrumbs*

**1** Stir the saffron into the wine in a small bowl and set aside. Heat the oil in a heavy-based saucepan and gently fry the onion and garlic for 5 minutes until softened. Stir in the rice and cook for another minute.

**2** Keeping the heat fairly high, add the wine and saffron mixture to the pan, stirring until it has all been absorbed. Gradually add the stock, stirring until all the liquid has been absorbed and the rice is cooked – this should take about 20 minutes.

**3** Stir in the prawns, chicken, petits pois and freshly grated Parmesan and stir well, cooking for 2–3 minutes. Season to taste with salt and pepper. Allow to cool slightly, then use two tablespoons to shape the mixture into 16 small croquettes.

**4** Mix the egg and milk in a shallow bowl. Spread out the breadcrumbs on a large flat plate. Dip the croquettes in the egg mixture, then roll them in the breadcrumbs to coat them. Heat the oil in a large frying pan. Shallow fry the croquettes for 4–5 minutes until crisp and golden brown. Drain on kitchen paper and serve hot, garnished with a sprig of flat leaf parsley.

# Sushi

This recipe shows one of the simplest forms of rolled sushi. You will need a bamboo mat (*makisu*) for the rolling process.

### *Makes 12 rolls or 72 slices*

INGREDIENTS
6 sheets yaki-nori seaweed

FOR THE FILLING
200 g/7 oz block raw tuna
200 g/7 oz block raw salmon
$^1/_2$ cucumber, quartered lengthways and seeds removed
wasabi paste (green horseradish)
gari (ginger pickles), to garnish
Japanese soy sauce, to serve

FOR THE SUSHI RICE
45 ml/3 tbsp rice vinegar
45 ml/3 tbsp granulated sugar
10 ml/2 tsp sea salt
350 g/12 oz/1$^3/_4$ cups Japanese rice, cooked

*yaki-nori seaweed*

*tuna*

*sea salt*

*salmon*

*cucumber*

*wasabi paste*

*rice vinegar*

*soy sauce*

*Japanese rice*

*sugar*

**1** To prepare the sushi rice, first make a dressing by heating the vinegar in a small saucepan, with a lid to keep in the strong vapours. Add the sugar and salt and dissolve. Allow to cool. Spread the cooked rice on to a mat or tray. Pour on the dressing and fluff with chopsticks or a fork. Leave aside to cool.

**2** Cut the nori in half lengthways. Place a sheet of nori, shiny side downwards, on a bamboo mat on a chopping board. Divide the cooked rice in half in its bowl, then mark each half into six, making 12 portions in all. Spread one portion of rice over the nori with your fingers, leaving a 1 cm/$^1/_2$ in space uncovered at the top and bottom of the nori.

**3** Cut the tuna, the salmon and the cucumber into four long sticks each. The sticks should be the same length as the long side of the nori and the ends should measure 1 cm/$^1/_2$ in square, Spread a little wasabi paste in a horizontal line along the middle of the rice and lay a stick of tuna on this.

## COOK'S TIP

Japanese ingredients can be found in specialist food shops. When you buy the raw fish, make sure that it is for *sashimi*, or for use as raw fish, which means it must be particularly clean and fresh. You may be unaccustomed to using some of the ingredients included in this recipe. Take care when using wasabi paste as it is extremely hot. It is also worth noting that Japanese soy sauce is different to the Chinese version, so do try to locate this for the recipe.

**4** Holding the mat and the edge of the nori nearest to you, roll up the nori and rice tightly into a tube with the tuna in the middle. Use the mat as a guide – do not roll it into the food.

**5** Carefully roll the sushi off the mat. Make 11 more rolls in the same way, four filled with salmon, four with tuna and four with cucumber. Do not use wasabi with the cucumber as the paste will make it discolour and soften. Use a wet knife to cut each roll into six slices and stand these on a platter. Wipe and rinse the knife occasionally between cuts. Garnish the sushi with gari, to refresh the palate between bites, and serve with soy sauce.

# Paella

Based on the classic Spanish recipe, seafood and bacon are cooked with aromatic saffron rice.

## Serves 6

INGREDIENTS

30 ml/2 tbsp olive oil
2 red peppers, seeded and roughly
    chopped
2 onions, roughly chopped
2 garlic cloves, crushed
115 g/4 oz rindless streaky bacon
    rashers, roughly chopped
350 g/12 oz/1¾ cups long grain rice
pinch of saffron strands
475 ml/16 fl oz/2 cups vegetable or
    chicken stock
300 ml/½ pint/1¼ cups dry white
    wine
350 g/12 oz ripe tomatoes
450 g/1 lb mixed cooked seafood,
    such as prawns, mussels and squid
115 g/4 oz/1 cup peas, thawed if
    frozen
45 ml/3 tbsp chopped fresh parsley
salt and freshly ground black pepper
whole cooked prawns and mussels in
    their shells, to garnish

garlic

tomatoes    onion    red peppers

mussels    white wine    parsley

peas    stock    cooked seafood

prawns    streaky bacon    saffron

1  Heat half the olive oil in a paella pan or large flameproof casserole. Cook the chopped peppers for about 3 minutes, remove with a slotted spoon and drain on kitchen paper. Add the rest of the oil and cook the onions, garlic and bacon for about 5 minutes, or until the onions have softened slightly, stirring regularly.

2  Add the rice and cook for 1 minute. Stir in the saffron, stock, wine and seasoning. Boil, then simmer, covered, for 12–15 minutes. Stir occasionally.

olive oil     long grain rice

3  Meanwhile, plunge the tomatoes into a bowl of boiling water, then into cold water and skin them. Quarter the tomatoes and scoop out the seeds. Roughly chop the flesh.

4  When the rice is cooked and most of the liquid has been absorbed, stir the tomatoes, seafood, peas and peppers into the mixture and heat gently, stirring occasionally, for 5 minutes or until piping hot. Stir in the parsley and adjust the seasoning before serving, garnished with the whole cooked prawns and mussels.

# Kedgeree

This classic rice recipe makes an ideal breakfast dish on a cold morning.

## Serves 6

INGREDIENTS
450 g/1 lb mixed smoked fish
300 ml/½ pint/1¼ cups milk
200 g/7 oz/1 cup long grain rice
1 slice of lemon
50 g/2 oz/¼ cup butter
5 ml/1 tsp medium curry powder
2.5 ml/½ tsp freshly grated nutmeg
15 ml/1 tbsp chopped fresh parsley
salt and freshly ground black pepper
flat leaf parsley sprigs, to garnish

TO SERVE
2 hard-boiled eggs, quartered
slices of hot buttered toast

smoked fish

parsley

nutmeg

long grain rice

lemon slice

butter

curry powder

milk

eggs

**1** Poach the uncooked smoked fish in milk for 10 minutes or until it flakes (see Cook's Tip). Drain off the milk and flake the fish. Mix with other smoked fish.

**2** Cook the rice in boiling water together with a slice of lemon for about 10 minutes until just cooked. Drain well.

## COOK'S TIP

You can use a variety of smoked fish. Cod and haddock are cold smoked and must be poached. Mackerel and trout are hot smoked and can be added next. If you are using smoked salmon, it can be added at this second stage even though it is cold smoked.

**3** Melt the butter in a large heavy-based saucepan and add the rice and fish. Shake the saucepan to mix all the ingredients together thoroughly.

**4** Stir in the curry powder, nutmeg, parsley and seasoning. Serve garnished with sprigs of parsley, quartered eggs and slices of hot buttered toast.

# Jambalaya

This Cajun dish comes from the Deep South of the USA. It contains a wonderful combination of rice, meat and fish, with a kick of chilli. If you like really spicy food, add a little more chilli powder.

*Serves 6*

INGREDIENTS

450 g/1 lb skinless, boneless chicken
   thighs
225 g/8 oz chorizo or spicy sausages
5 celery sticks
1 red pepper, seeded
1 green pepper, seeded
about 30 ml/2 tbsp oil
2 onions, roughly chopped
2 garlic cloves, crushed
10 ml/2 tsp mild chilli powder
2.5 ml/$^1\!/_2$ tsp ground ginger
300 g/11 oz/1$^2\!/_3$ cups long grain rice
900 ml/1$^1\!/_2$ pints/3$^3\!/_4$ cups chicken
   stock
175 g/6 oz peeled cooked prawns
salt and freshly ground black pepper
12 cooked prawns in shells, with
   heads removed, to garnish

*peeled prawns*   *chorizo*   *celery*

*chicken thighs*   *long grain rice*   *ground ginger*

*cooked prawns*   *oil*   *chicken stock*

*garlic*   *onions*

*green and red peppers*   *chilli powder*

**1** Cut the chicken and chorizo or spicy sausages into small, bite-size pieces. Cut the celery and peppers into thin 5 cm/2 in strips and set aside.

**2** Heat the oil in a very large frying pan or large saucepan and cook the chicken until golden. Remove with a slotted spoon and drain on kitchen paper. Cook the chorizo for 2 minutes and drain on kitchen paper.

**3** Add the celery and peppers and cook for 3–4 minutes, until the vegetables begin to soften and turn golden. Drain on kitchen paper. Add a little more oil to the pan, if needed, and cook the onions and garlic for 3 minutes.

**4** Stir in the chilli powder and ginger and cook for a further 1 minute.

**5** Add the rice. Cook for 1 minute until it begins to look translucent. Stir in the stock, replace the chicken and bring to the boil. Cover, then simmer for 12–15 minutes, stirring occasionally, until the rice is tender and the liquid has been absorbed. Add a little more water, if necessary, during cooking.

**6** Gently stir the chorizo, peppers, celery and peeled prawns into the rice. Cook over a low heat, turning the mixture over with a large spoon, until piping hot. Adjust the seasoning and serve, garnished with the whole prawns.

# Middle-eastern Fish with Rice

This Arabic fish dish, *Sayadieh*, is very popular in the Lebanon.

*Serves 4-6*

INGREDIENTS
juice of 1 lemon
45 ml/3 tbsp oil
900 g/2 lb cod steaks
4 large onions, chopped
5 ml/1 tsp ground cumin
2-3 saffron strands
1 litre/1¾ pints/4 cups fish stock
450 g/1 lb/2¼ cups long grain rice
50 g/2 oz/⅔ cup pine nuts, lightly
    toasted
salt and freshly ground black pepper
fresh parsley, to garnish

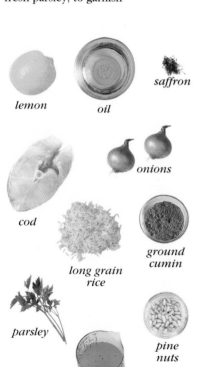

lemon  oil  *saffron*

*onions*

*cod*  *ground cumin*

*long grain rice*

*parsley*  *pine nuts*

*fish stock*

**1** Mix together the lemon juice and 15 ml/1 tbsp of the oil in a shallow dish. Add the fish steaks, turning to coat thoroughly, then cover and leave to marinate for 30 minutes. Heat the remaining oil in a large saucepan or flameproof casserole and fry the onions for about 5–6 minutes until golden, stirring occasionally.

**2** Drain the fish, reserving the marinade, and add to the pan. Fry for 1–2 minutes each side until lightly golden, then add the cumin, saffron strands and a little salt and pepper.

**3** Pour in the fish stock and the reserved marinade and bring to the boil. Leave to simmer gently over a low heat for about 5 minutes until the fish is almost cooked.

## VARIATION

You can try this recipe using some other firm-fleshed fish, if you like, such as swordfish. You can also use any type of long grain rice. Brown rice would make a particularly healthy option. If using, add some extra water with the stock and top up if necessary.

**4** Transfer the fish to a plate and add the rice to the stock. Bring to the boil and then reduce the heat and simmer gently over a low heat for 15 minutes until the stock has nearly all been absorbed. Add extra water if necessary, a little at a time.

**5** Arrange the fish on the rice and cover. Steam over a low heat for a further 10–15 minutes. Transfer the fish to a plate, then spoon the rice on to a large flat dish and arrange the fish on top. Sprinkle with toasted pine nuts and garnish with fresh parsley.

# Indonesian Fried Rice

This fried rice dish makes an ideal supper on its own or even as an accompaniment. It is a very quick meal to prepare as the rice is already cooked.

## Serves 4

INGREDIENTS
4 shallots, roughly chopped
1 red chilli, seeded and chopped
1 garlic clove, chopped
thin sliver of dried shrimp paste
45 ml/3 tbsp oil
225 g/8 oz boneless lean pork, cut into fine strips
200 g/7 oz/1 cup long grain rice, boiled and cooled
3–4 spring onions, thinly sliced
115 g/4 oz cooked peeled prawns
30 ml/2 tbsp sweet soy sauce
chopped fresh coriander and fine cucumber shreds, to garnish

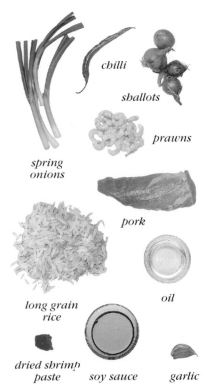

chilli

shallots

prawns

spring onions

pork

long grain rice

oil

dried shrimp paste

soy sauce

garlic

**1** In a mortar pound the shallots, chilli, garlic and shrimp paste with a pestle until they form a paste.

**2** Heat a wok until hot, add 30 ml/ 2 tbsp of the oil and swirl it around. Add the pork and stir-fry for 2–3 minutes. Remove the pork from the wok, set aside and keep hot.

**3** Add the remaining oil to the wok. When hot, add the spiced shallot paste and stir-fry for about 30 seconds.

**4** Reduce the heat. Add the rice, spring onions and prawns. Stir-fry for 2–3 minutes. Add the pork and sprinkle over the soy sauce. Stir-fry until piping hot. Serve garnished with the chopped coriander and cucumber shreds.

# Chicken Paella

There are many variations on the basic paella recipe. Any seasonal vegetables can be added, as can mussels and other seafood.

## Serves 4

INGREDIENTS
4 chicken legs (thighs and
    drumsticks)
60 ml/4 tbsp olive oil
1 large onion, finely chopped
1 garlic clove, crushed
5 ml/1 tsp ground turmeric
115 g/4 oz chorizo or smoked ham
225 g/8 oz/1¼ cups long
    grain rice
600 ml/1 pint/2½ cups chicken stock
4 tomatoes, peeled, seeded and
    chopped
1 red pepper, seeded and sliced
115 g/4 oz/1 cup frozen peas
salt and freshly ground black pepper

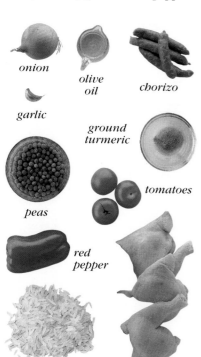

*onion*

*olive
oil*

*chorizo*

*garlic*

*ground
turmeric*

*tomatoes*

*peas*

*red
pepper*

*long grain rice*

*chicken*

*chicken
stock*

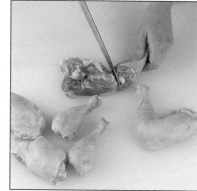

**1** Preheat the oven to 180°C/350°F/ Gas 4. Cut the chicken legs in half.

**2** Heat the oil in a 30 cm/12 in paella pan or large flameproof casserole and brown the chicken pieces on both sides. Add the onion and garlic and stir in the turmeric. Cook for 2 minutes.

**3** Slice the chorizo or dice the ham and add to the pan, together with the rice and stock. Bring to the boil and season to taste. Remove from the hob, cover and bake in the oven for about 15 minutes.

**4** Remove from the oven and add the tomatoes, red pepper and frozen peas. Return to the oven and cook for a further 10–15 minutes or until the chicken is tender and the rice has absorbed the stock. Serve hot.

# Poussins with Dirty Rice

In this Cajun dish, the rice is called "dirty" not because of its colour but because the local term for jazz is "dirty music", and the rice here will certainly be jazzed up.

## Serves 4

INGREDIENTS

60 ml/4 tbsp oil
25 g/1 oz/¼ cup plain flour
50 g/2 oz/¼ cup butter
1 large onion, chopped
2 celery sticks, chopped
1 green pepper, seeded and diced
2 garlic cloves, crushed
200 g/7 oz minced pork
225 g/8 oz chicken livers, trimmed and sliced
dash of Tabasco sauce
300 ml/½ pint/1¼ cups chicken stock
4 spring onions, shredded
45 ml/3 tbsp chopped fresh parsley
225 g/8 oz/1¼ cups long grain rice, freshly cooked
2 bay leaves, halved
4 poussins
25 g/1 oz/2 tbsp butter, for basting
1 lemon
salt and freshly ground black pepper

**1** Heat half the oil in a small heavy saucepan and stir in the flour to make a roux. When it is a chestnut-brown colour, remove the pan from the heat and place it immediately on a cold surface. Heat the remaining oil with 50 g/2 oz/¼ cup butter in a frying pan and stir-fry the onion, celery and pepper for 5 minutes.

**2** Add the garlic and pork and stir-fry for 5 minutes, breaking up the pork with a spoon so that it cooks evenly. Add the chicken livers and fry for 3 minutes until they have all changed colour. Season and add a dash of Tabasco sauce.

**3** Stir the roux into the stir-fried mixture, then gradually add the stock. When the mixture bubbles, cover and simmer for 30 minutes, stirring occasionally. Then uncover and cook for a further 15 minutes, stirring frequently.

**4** Preheat the oven to 200°C/400°F/ Gas 6. Mix the spring onions and parsley into the meat mixture and stir it all into the cooked rice. Put ½ bay leaf and about 15 ml/1 tbsp of the rice mixture into each poussin. Rub the outsides with the remaining butter and season well.

oil

flour

butter

garlic

Tabasco sauce

onion

chicken stock

celery

minced pork

bay leaves

green pepper

parsley

chicken livers

spring onions

long grain rice

poussins

lemon

 Put the birds on a rack in a roasting tin, squeeze the juice from the lemon over them and roast in the oven for 35–40 minutes, basting twice with the pan juices. Put the remaining rice mixture into a shallow ovenproof dish, cover it and place on a low shelf in the oven for the last 15–20 minutes of the birds' cooking time. Serve the birds on a bed of dirty rice with the roasting pan juices (drained of fat) poured over.

## COOK'S TIP
You can substitute quails for the poussins, in which case offer two per person and stuff each little bird with 10 ml/2 tsp of the dirty rice before roasting for about 20 minutes.

# Thai Fried Rice

This hot and spicy dish is easy to prepare and makes a meal in itself. The delicate balance of flavours is exquisite.

*Serves 4*

INGREDIENTS

225 g/8 oz/1¼ cups jasmine rice
45 ml/3 tbsp oil
1 onion, chopped
1 small red pepper, seeded and cut
    into 2 cm/¾ in cubes
350 g/12 oz skinless, boneless
    chicken breasts, cut into
    2 cm/¾ in cubes
1 garlic clove, crushed
15 ml/1 tbsp mild curry paste
2.5 ml/½ tsp paprika
2.5 ml/½ tsp ground turmeric
30 ml/2 tbsp Thai fish sauce
    (nam pla)
2 eggs, beaten
salt and freshly ground black pepper
fried fresh basil leaves, to garnish

*jasmine rice*

*Thai fish sauce*

*oil*

*onion*

*red pepper*

*turmeric*

*curry paste*

*paprika*

*garlic*

*eggs*

*chicken*

**1** Place the rice in a sieve and wash well under cold running water. Put the rice in a heavy-based pan with 1.5 litres/2½ pints/6¼ cups boiling water. Return to the boil, then simmer, uncovered, for 8–10 minutes. Drain well. Spread out the grains on a tray and leave to cool.

**2** Heat a wok until hot. Add 30 ml/2 tbsp of the oil and swirl it around. Add the onion and red pepper and stir-fry for 1 minute until the onion just begins to soften slightly.

**3** Add the chicken, garlic, curry paste and spices and stir-fry for 4–5 minutes, stirring well to evenly distribute the flavours and the paste.

**4** Reduce the heat to medium, add the cooled rice, fish sauce and seasoning. Stir-fry for 2–3 minutes until the rice is very hot.

**5** Make a well in the centre of the rice and add the remaining oil. When hot, add the beaten eggs, leave to cook for about 2 minutes until lightly set, then stir into the rice.

**6** Scatter over the fried basil leaves and serve at once.

## VARIATION
Add 50 g/2 oz/¼ cup frozen peas to the chicken in step 3, if you wish.

# Chicken Biryani

In India, this dish is mainly prepared for important occasions, and is truly fit for royalty. Every cook has a subtle variation, which is kept a closely guarded secret.

## Serves 4-6

INGREDIENTS

1.4 kg/3 lb chicken breast, skinless, boneless, cut into large pieces
60 ml/4 tbsp biryani masala paste
2 green chillies, chopped
15 ml/1 tbsp crushed fresh ginger
4 garlic cloves, crushed
50 g/2 oz fresh coriander, chopped
6-8 fresh mint leaves, chopped or 5 ml/1 tsp mint sauce
150 ml/¼ pint/⅔ cup natural yogurt, beaten
30 ml/2 tbsp tomato purée
4 onions, finely sliced, deep fried and crushed
salt, to taste
450 g/1 lb/2¼ cups basmati rice, washed and drained
5 ml/1 tsp black cumin seeds
1 piece cinnamon stick, 5 cm/2 in long
4 green cardamoms
2 black cardamoms
oil, for shallow frying
4 large potatoes, peeled and quartered
350 ml/12 fl oz/1½ cups mixed milk and water
1 sachet saffron powder, mixed with 90 ml/6 tbsp milk
30 ml/2 tbsp ghee or unsalted butter

FOR THE GARNISH

ghee or unsalted butter, for shallow-frying
50 g/2 oz/½ cup cashew nuts
50 g/2 oz/⅓ cup sultanas
2 hard-boiled eggs, quartered
deep fried onion slices

**1** Mix the chicken with the next 10 ingredients in a large bowl and allow to marinate for about 2 hours. Place in a large heavy pan and cook gently for about 10 minutes. Set aside.

**2** Bring a large saucepan of water to the boil. Add the rice, cumin seeds, cinnamon stick and cardamoms, remove from the heat and soak for 5 minutes. Drain well. Remove the cinnamon and cardamoms at this stage, if you like.

**3** Heat the oil for shallow frying in a frying pan and fry the potatoes until they are evenly browned on all sides. Drain the potatoes on kitchen paper and set aside until needed.

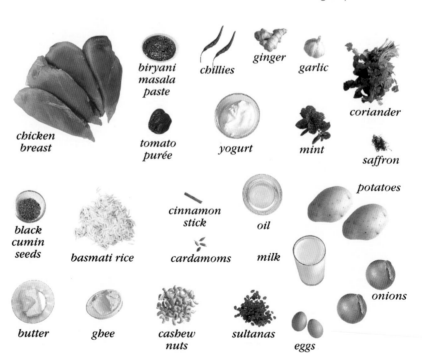

*chicken breast*  *biryani masala paste*  *chillies*  *ginger*  *garlic*  *coriander*

*tomato purée*  *yogurt*  *mint*  *saffron*

*black cumin seeds*  *basmati rice*  *cinnamon stick*  *oil*  *potatoes*

*cardamoms*  *milk*

*butter*  *ghee*  *cashew nuts*  *sultanas*  *eggs*  *onions*

**4** Place half the rice on top of the chicken mixture in the pan in an even layer. Top with an even layer of potatoes. Put the remaining rice mixture on top of the potatoes and spread out to make an even layer. Sprinkle the milk and water mixture all over the top of the rice.

**5** Make holes on the top with the handle of a spoon and pour a little saffron milk into each one. Add a few knobs of ghee or butter, cover and cook over a low heat for 35–45 minutes.

**6** While the biryani is cooking, make the garnish. Heat a little ghee or butter in a frying pan and fry the cashew nuts and sultanas until the sultanas swell. Drain and set aside. When the biryani is ready, gently toss the rice, chicken and potatoes together. Garnish with the nut mixture, hard-boiled eggs and onion slices and serve hot.

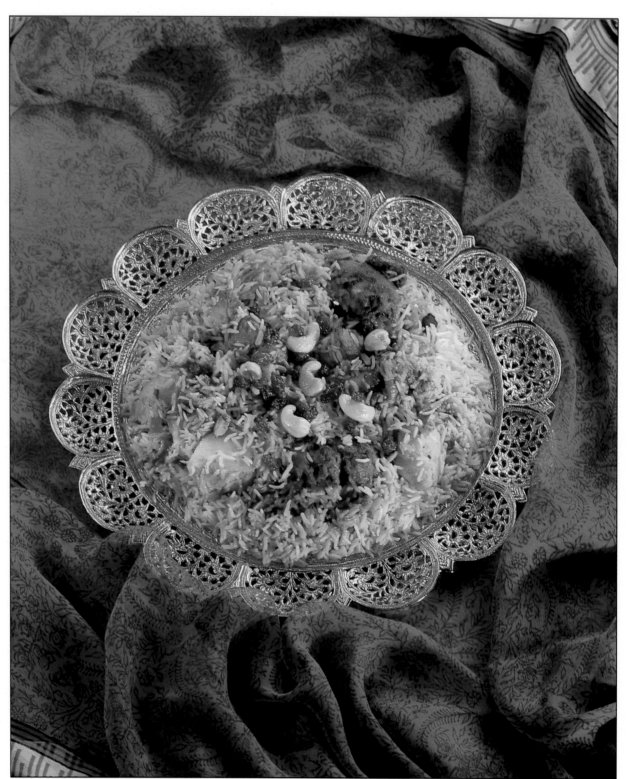

# Nasi Goreng

This dish is originally from Thailand, but it can easily be adapted by adding any cooked ingredients that are at hand. Crispy prawn crackers make an ideal accompaniment.

## Serves 4

INGREDIENTS

225 g/8 oz/1¼ cups long grain rice
2 eggs
30 ml/2 tbsp oil
1 green chilli
2 spring onions, roughly chopped
2 garlic cloves, crushed
225 g/8 oz cooked chicken
225 g/8 oz cooked prawns, peeled
45 ml/3 tbsp dark soy sauce
spring onion shreds, to garnish
prawn crackers, to serve

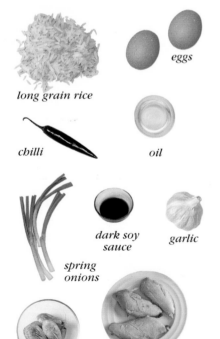

long grain rice

chilli

oil

dark soy
sauce

garlic

spring
onions

prawns

cooked chicken

eggs

**1** Rinse and drain the rice and then place in a saucepan together with 600 ml/1 pint/2½ cups water. Bring to the boil, cover with a tight-fitting lid and cook over a low heat for about 10–12 minutes. Rinse the rice with cold water through a sieve to cool it.

**2** Lightly beat the eggs. Heat 15 ml/ 1 tbsp of oil in a small frying pan and swirl in the beaten egg. When cooked on one side, flip over and cook on the other side, remove from the pan and leave to cool. Cut the omelette into thin strips and leave aside.

**3** Carefully remove the seeds from the chilli and chop finely, wearing rubber gloves to protect your hands if necessary. Always keep hands away from eyes when chopping chillies. Place the spring onions, chilli and garlic in a food processor and blend to a paste.

**4** Heat the wok, and then add the remaining oil. When the oil is hot, add the paste and stir-fry for 1 minute.

**5** Add the cooked chicken and prawns and stir-fry until hot, making sure that the paste coats the chicken and prawns evenly.

**6** Add the cooked rice and stir-fry for 3–4 minutes until piping hot. Stir in the omelette strips and soy sauce and garnish with spring onion shreds. Serve with prawn crackers.

# Red Beans and Rice with Salt Pork

This classic Cajun dish is worth making in large quantities because of the long cooking time. It makes a splendid supper-party dish served with grilled sausages and a green salad.

## *Serves 8–10*

INGREDIENTS

500 g/1¼ lb/2 cups dried red kidney beans, soaked in cold water overnight, rinsed and drained
2 bay leaves
30 ml/2 tbsp oil, bacon fat or lard
1 onion, chopped
2 garlic cloves, finely chopped
2 celery sticks, sliced
225 g/8 oz piece of salt pork or raw ham
450 g/1 lb/2¼ cups long grain rice
45 ml/3 tbsp chopped fresh parsley
salt and freshly ground black pepper

*red kidney beans*

*bay leaves*

*oil*

*onion*

*garlic*

*celery*

*parsley*

*long grain rice*

*ham*

**1** Place the beans in a large saucepan with cold water to cover. Boil rapidly for 10 minutes. Drain and rinse the beans and the pan. Return the beans to the pan, add the bay leaves and cover with cold water. Bring to the boil, reduce the heat and simmer for 30 minutes.

**4** Measure the rice into a pan with a cup and add 750 ml/1¼ pints/3 cups water. Stir in 5 ml/1 tsp salt. Bring to the boil, stirring occasionally, then cover the pan with a tight-fitting lid and leave to cook over a very low heat for about 15 minutes. Without lifting the lid, turn off the heat and leave the rice for a further 5–10 minutes.

## COOK'S TIP

Red kidney beans carry dangerous toxins so it is very important that they are washed, soaked overnight and fast boiled before cooking.

**2** Meanwhile heat the oil, fat or lard in a frying pan and cook the onion, garlic and celery gently, stirring frequently, until the onion is soft and translucent. Add them to the beans.

**5** Lift the piece of salt pork or ham out from among the beans and dice it, removing the fat and rind.

**3** Add the piece of salt pork or ham to the beans, pushing well down. Bring back to the boil and simmer, topping up the water as necessary, for 45 minutes until the beans are very tender. Add salt, if necessary, 15–20 minutes before the end of the cooking time.

**6** Drain the beans and adjust the seasoning. Mix the meat through the beans. Fluff up the rice and stir in the parsley. Serve with the beans on top.

# Lamb Pilau

In the Caribbean rice is often cooked with meat and coconut milk, giving a deliciously rich and creamy texture. Sweet potato crisps would make an ideal accompaniment, and are easily made by deep frying thin slices of the vegetable until crisp.

## Serves 4

INGREDIENTS

450 g/1 lb stewing lamb
15 ml/1 tbsp curry powder
1 onion, chopped
2 garlic cloves, crushed
2.5 ml/½ tsp dried thyme
2.5 ml/½ tsp dried oregano
1 fresh or dried chilli, seeded and
   chopped
25 g/1 oz/2 tbsp butter or margarine,
   plus extra for serving
600 ml/1 pint/2½ cups beef or
   chicken stock or coconut milk
5 ml/1 tsp freshly ground black
   pepper
2 tomatoes, chopped
10 ml/2 tsp granulated sugar
30 ml/2 tbsp chopped spring onions
450 g/1 lb/2¼ cups basmati rice
spring onion strips, to garnish

**1** Cut the meat into cubes, discarding any excess fat and gristle. Place in a shallow glass or china dish.

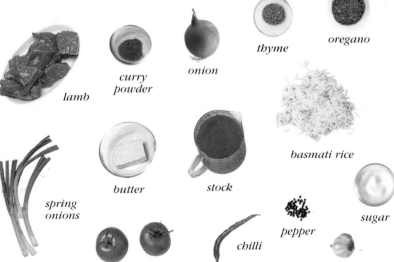

lamb

curry powder

onion

thyme

oregano

basmati rice

spring onions

butter

stock

sugar

pepper

chilli

garlic

tomatoes

**2** Sprinkle with the curry powder, onion, garlic, herbs and chilli. Stir well. Cover loosely with clear film and leave to marinate in a cool place for 1 hour. Melt the butter or margarine in a saucepan and fry the lamb on all sides for 5–10 minutes. Add the stock or coconut milk. Bring to the boil, lower the heat and simmer for 35 minutes or until the meat is tender.

**3** Add the black pepper, tomatoes, sugar, spring onions and rice, stir well and reduce the heat. Make sure that the rice is covered by 2.5 cm/1 in of liquid and add a little water if necessary. Simmer the pilau for 25 minutes or until the rice is cooked, then stir a little extra butter or margarine into the rice before serving. Garnish with spring onion strips.

# Wild Rice and Turkey Salad

A delicious and healthy salad that makes a perfect light lunch or supper dish. For a softer texture but a similar flavour, use a mixture of wild rice and long grain rice and reduce the cooking time a little.

## Serves 4

INGREDIENTS
175 g/6 oz/³/₄ cup wild rice
2 celery stalks, thinly sliced
2 spring onions, chopped
115 g/4 oz/1 cup small button
    mushrooms, quartered
450 g/1 lb cold cooked turkey breast,
    diced
120 ml/4 fl oz/¹/₂ cup vinaigrette
    dressing, made with walnut oil
salt
4 fresh thyme sprigs

TO SERVE
2 pears, peeled, halved and cored
25 g/1 oz/3 tbsp walnut pieces,
    toasted

**1** Pour 1 litre/1³/₄ pints/4 cups cold water into a saucepan and add a pinch of salt. Bring to the boil. Add the wild rice to the pan and bring back to the boil. Cook for 45–50 minutes, until tender but firm and the grains have begun to split open. Drain well and leave to cool.

celery

wild rice

turkey breast

spring onions

pears

thyme

mushrooms

walnut pieces

## VARIATION
You can use chicken instead of turkey breast with any vinaigrette dressing. Toast a selection of nuts for a different flavour, if you like.

**2** Combine the wild rice with the celery, spring onions, mushrooms and cooked turkey in a bowl.

**3** Add the dressing and thyme and toss well together. Thinly slice the pear halves lengthways without cutting through the stalk end and spread the slices like a fan. Divide the salad among 4 plates. Garnish each with a fanned pear half and toasted walnuts.

## Oriental Fried Rice

This is a great way to use leftover cooked rice. Make sure the rice is very cold before attempting to fry it as warm rice will become soggy. Some supermarkets sell frozen cooked rice.

### Serves 4-6

INGREDIENTS

75 ml/5 tbsp oil

115 g/4 oz shallots, halved and thinly sliced

3 garlic cloves, crushed

1 red chilli, seeded and finely chopped

6 spring onions, finely chopped

1 red pepper, seeded and finely chopped

225 g/8 oz white cabbage, finely shredded

175 g/6 oz cucumber, finely chopped

50 g/2 oz/¹/₂ cup peas, thawed if frozen

3 eggs, beaten

5 ml/1 tsp tomato purée

30 ml/2 tbsp lime juice

1.5 ml/¹/₄ tsp Tabasco sauce

225 g/8 oz/1¹/₄ cups long grain rice, cooked and cooled

115 g/4 oz/1 cup cashew nuts, roughly chopped

about 30 ml/2 tbsp chopped fresh coriander, plus extra to garnish

salt and freshly ground black pepper

oil

shallots

garlic

red
chilli

cucumber

eggs

peas

tomato
purée

cashew
nuts

long grain
rice

spring
onions

coriander

lime
juice

Tabasco
sauce

red
pepper

white
cabbage

**1** Heat half the oil in a large non-stick frying pan or wok and cook the shallots until very crisp and golden. Remove with a slotted spoon and drain well on kitchen paper.

**2** Add the rest of the oil to the pan. Cook the garlic and chilli for 1 minute. Add the spring onions and pepper and cook for a further 3–4 minutes.

**3** Add the cabbage, cucumber and peas and cook for a further 2 minutes.

**4** Make a gap in the pan and add the beaten eggs. Scramble the eggs, stirring occasionally, and then stir them into the vegetables.

**5** Add the tomato purée, lime juice and Tabasco and stir to combine.

**6** Increase the heat and add the rice, cashew nuts and coriander with plenty of seasoning. Stir-fry for 3–4 minutes, until piping hot. Serve garnished with the crisp shallots and extra fresh coriander.

# Lentils and Rice

Lentils are cooked with whole and ground spices, potatoes, rice and onions here to produce an authentic Indian-style dish, which makes a satisfying light but wholesome meal.

## Serves 4

INGREDIENTS
150 g/5 oz/²/₃ cup red split lentils
115 g/4 oz/²/₃ cup basmati rice
1 large potato
1 large onion
30 ml/2 tbsp oil
4 whole cloves
1.5 ml/¹/₄ tsp cumin seeds
1.5 ml/¹/₄ tsp ground turmeric
10 ml/2 tsp salt

basmati
rice

oil

cumin
seeds

ground
turmeric

red split
lentils

potato

salt

cloves    onion

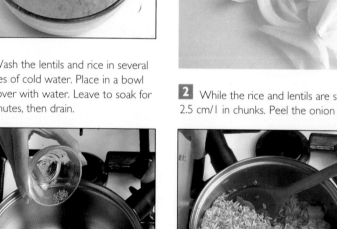

**1** Wash the lentils and rice in several changes of cold water. Place in a bowl and cover with water. Leave to soak for 15 minutes, then drain.

**2** While the rice and lentils are soaking, peel the potato and rinse well. Cut it into 2.5 cm/1 in chunks. Peel the onion and cut the onion into thin slices.

**3** Heat the oil in a large heavy-based saucepan and fry the cloves and cumin seeds for 2 minutes until the seeds are beginning to splutter.

**4** Add the onion and potatoes and fry for 5 minutes until slightly browned. Add the lentils and rice, with turmeric and salt and fry for 3 minutes.

**5** Pour 475 ml/16 fl oz/2 cups water into a saucepan. Bring to the boil, cover tightly and simmer for 15–20 minutes, until all the water has been absorbed and the potatoes are tender. Leave to stand, covered, for about 10 minutes, and then serve.

# Vegetable Kedgeree

Crunchy French beans and mushrooms are the star ingredients in this vegetarian version of a rice dish traditionally made with fish as well as egg.

## Serves 2

INGREDIENTS

115 g/4 oz/²/₃ cup basmati rice
3 eggs
175 g/6 oz French beans, trimmed
50 g/2 oz/4 tbsp butter
1 onion, finely chopped
225 g/8 oz/2 cups brown cap
    mushrooms, quartered
30 ml/2 tbsp single cream
15 ml/1 tbsp chopped fresh parsley
salt and freshly ground black pepper

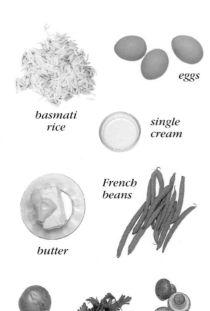

basmati
rice

eggs

single
cream

French
beans

butter

onion

parsley

brown cap
mushrooms

**1** Wash the rice several times under cold running water. Drain thoroughly. Bring a pan of water to the boil, add the rice and cook for 10–12 minutes until tender. Drain thoroughly.

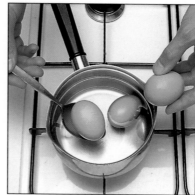

**2** Half fill a second pan with water, add the eggs and bring to the boil. Lower the heat and simmer for 8 minutes. Drain the eggs, cool them under running cold water, then remove the shells and rinse.

**3** Bring another pan of water to the boil and cook the French beans for about 5 minutes. Drain, refresh under cold running water, then drain again.

**4** Melt the butter in a large frying pan. Add the onion and mushrooms. Cook for 2–3 minutes over a moderate heat.

**5** Add the French beans and rice to the onion mixture. Stir lightly to mix. Cook for 2 minutes. Cut the hard-boiled eggs in wedges and carefully add them to the pan.

**6** Stir in the cream and parsley, taking care not to break up the eggs. Reheat the kedgeree, but do not allow it to boil. Season with salt and pepper and serve at once.

# Vegetable Pilau

A delicious vegetable rice dish that also goes well
with most Indian meat dishes.

## *Serves 4-6*

INGREDIENTS

225 g/8 oz/1¼ cups basmati rice
30 ml/2 tbsp oil
2.5 ml/½ tsp cumin seeds
2 bay leaves
4 green cardamom pods
4 cloves
1 onion, finely chopped
1 carrot, finely chopped
50 g/2 oz/½ cup peas, thawed if
 frozen
50 g/2 oz/⅓ cup sweetcorn kernels,
 thawed if frozen
25 g/1 oz/¼ cup cashew nuts, lightly
 fried
1.5 ml/¼ tsp ground coriander
1.5 ml/¼ tsp ground cumin
salt

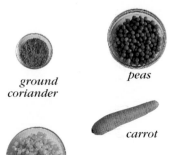
*ground
coriander*

*peas*

*sweetcorn*

*carrot*

*cumin seeds*

*oil*

*bay leaves*

*onion*

*ground
cumin*

*cardamom
pods*

*cloves*

*cashew
nuts*

*basmati
rice*

**1** Wash the basmati rice in several
changes of cold water. Put into a bowl
and cover with cold water. Leave to
soak for 30 minutes.

**2** Heat the oil in a large frying pan and
fry the cumin seeds for 2 minutes. Add
the bay leaves, cardamoms and cloves
and fry for 2 minutes.

**3** Add the onion and fry for 5 minutes
until lightly browned.

**4** Stir in the carrot and cook for
3–4 minutes.

**5** Drain the rice and add to the pan
with the peas, sweetcorn and cashew
nuts. Fry for 4–5 minutes.

**6** Pour in 475 ml/16 fl oz/2 cups cold
water, then add the remaining spices
and salt to taste. Bring to the boil, cover,
then simmer for about 15 minutes over
a low heat until all the water is
absorbed. Leave to stand, covered, for
10 minutes before serving.

## VARIATION

You can add your favourite
vegetables to this recipe, such as
potatoes, if you like, although this
particular vegetable will require a
longer cooking time.

# Stuffed Vegetables

Vegetables such as peppers make wonderful containers for savoury fillings. Instead of sticking to one type of vegetable serve a selection. Thick, creamy Greek yogurt is the ideal accompaniment.

## Serves 3-6

INGREDIENTS
1 aubergine
1 large green pepper
2 large tomatoes
1 large onion, chopped
2 garlic cloves, crushed
45 ml/3 tbsp olive oil
200 g/7 oz/1 cup brown rice
600 ml/1 pint/2¹/₂ cups vegetable stock
75 g/3 oz/1 cup pine nuts
50 g/2 oz/¹/₃ cup currants
45 ml/3 tbsp chopped fresh dill
45 ml/3 tbsp chopped fresh parsley
15 ml/1 tbsp chopped fresh mint
extra olive oil, to sprinkle
salt and freshly ground black pepper
Greek yogurt and fresh dill sprigs, to serve

**1** Halve the aubergine, scoop out the flesh with a sharp knife and chop finely. Salt the insides and leave to drain upside down for 20 minutes while you prepare the other ingredients. Halve the pepper, seed and core.

**2** Cut the tops from the tomatoes, scoop out the insides and chop roughly along with the tomato tops. Set the tomato shells aside. Fry the onion, garlic and chopped aubergine in the oil for 10 minutes, then stir in the rice and cook for 2 minutes. Add the tomato flesh, stock, pine nuts, currants and seasoning. Bring to the boil, cover and lower the heat. Simmer for 15 minutes then stir in the herbs.

*aubergine*   *garlic*   *tomatoes*   *yogurt*

*green pepper*   *onion*

*olive oil*   *brown rice*   *pine nuts*   *vegetable stock*

*dill*   *parsley*   *mint*   *currants*

**3** Preheat the oven to 190°C/375°F/Gas 5. Blanch the aubergine and green pepper halves in boiling water for about 3 minutes, then drain them upside down on kitchen paper.

**4** Spoon the rice filling into all six vegetable containers and place on a lightly greased shallow baking dish. Drizzle some olive oil over the stuffed vegetables and bake for 25–30 minutes. Serve hot, topped with spoonfuls of yogurt and the dill sprigs.

# Pilau with Omelette Rolls and Nuts

A wonderful mixture of textures – soft fluffy rice with crunchy nuts and omelette rolls.

## Serves 2

INGREDIENTS

175 g/6 oz/scant 1 cup basmati rice
15 ml/1 tbsp sunflower oil
1 small onion, chopped
1 red pepper, finely diced
350 ml/12 fl oz/1½ cups hot
    vegetable stock
2 eggs
25 g/1 oz/¼ cup salted peanuts
15 ml/1 tbsp soy sauce
salt and freshly ground black pepper
fresh parsley sprigs, to garnish

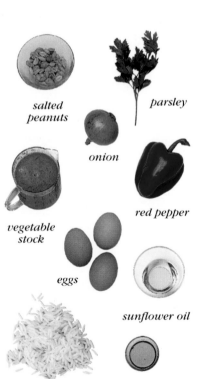

*salted peanuts*

*parsley*

*onion*

*red pepper*

*vegetable stock*

*eggs*

*sunflower oil*

*soy sauce*

*basmati rice*

**1** Wash the rice several times under cold running water. Drain thoroughly. Heat half the oil in a large frying pan. Fry the onion and pepper for 2–3 minutes, then stir in the rice and stock, bring to the boil and cook for 10–12 minutes until the rice is tender.

**2** Meanwhile, beat the eggs lightly with salt and pepper to taste. Heat the remaining oil in a second large frying pan. Pour in the eggs and tilt the pan to cover the base thinly. Cook the omelette for 1 minute, then flip it over and cook the other side for 1 minute.

**3** Slide the omelette on to a clean board and roll it up tightly. Cut the omelette roll into 8 slices.

**4** Stir the peanuts and the soy sauce into the pilau and add black pepper to taste. Turn the pilau into a serving dish, arrange the omelette rolls on top and garnish with the parsley. Serve at once.

# Fruity Rice Salad

An appetizing and colourful rice salad combining many different flavours, ideal for a packed lunch.

*Serves 4-6*

INGREDIENTS

225 g/8 oz/1 cup mixed brown and
    wild rice
1 yellow pepper, seeded and diced
1 bunch spring onions, chopped
3 celery sticks, chopped
1 large beefsteak tomato, chopped
2 green-skinned eating apples,
    chopped
175 g/6 oz/³/₄ cup ready-to-eat dried
    apricots, chopped
115 g/4 oz/²/₃ cup raisins

FOR THE DRESSING

30 ml/2 tbsp unsweetened apple
    juice
30 ml/2 tbsp dry sherry
30 ml/2 tbsp light soy sauce
dash of Tabasco sauce
30 ml/2 tbsp chopped fresh parsley
15 ml/1 tbsp chopped fresh rosemary
salt and freshly ground black pepper

*celery*

*mixed brown
and wild rice*

*spring
onions*

*beefsteak
tomato*

*apricots*

*apple juice*

*soy sauce*

*raisins*  *rosemary*  *parsley*

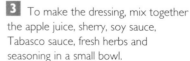
*sherry*  *Tabasco
sauce*  *eating
apples*  *yellow
pepper*

**1** Cook the rice in a large saucepan of lightly salted, boiling water for about 35 minutes until tender. Rinse the rice under cold running water to cool quickly and drain thoroughly.

**2** Place the pepper, spring onions, celery, tomato, apples, apricots, raisins and the cooked rice in a large serving bowl and mix well.

**3** To make the dressing, mix together the apple juice, sherry, soy sauce, Tabasco sauce, fresh herbs and seasoning in a small bowl.

**4** Pour the dressing over the rice mixture and toss the ingredients together to mix. Serve immediately or cover and chill in the fridge until ready to serve.

# Risotto with Asparagus

A fresh and delicious risotto is one of the nicest classic rice dishes. This recipe makes an elegant meal when asparagus is in season.

## Serves 4-5

INGREDIENTS

225 g/8 oz asparagus, lower stalks
    peeled
750 ml/1¼ pints/3 cups vegetable or
    meat stock, preferably home-made
65 g/2½ oz/5 tbsp butter
1 small onion, finely chopped
400 g/14 oz/2 cups risotto rice
75 g/3 oz/1 cup freshly grated
    Parmesan cheese
salt and freshly ground black pepper

*stock*

*asparagus*

*butter*

*risotto rice*

*onion*

*Parmesan cheese*

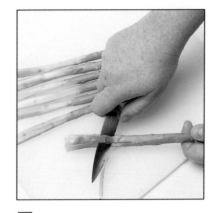

**1** Boil 750 ml/1¼ pints/3 cups water in a large saucepan and blanch the asparagus for 5 minutes. Remove, reserving the cooking water and rinse under cold water. Drain and cut each one diagonally into 4 cm/1½ in pieces, separating the tip and next-highest sections from the stalks. Place the stock in a saucepan with 600 ml/1 pint/2½ cups of the asparagus cooking water. Heat the liquid to simmering, and keep it hot until it is needed.

**2** Heat two-thirds of the butter in a large heavy frying pan or casserole. Add the onion and cook until it is soft and golden. Stir in the asparagus stalks. Cook for 2–3 minutes. Add the rice, mixing well to coat the grains with butter. Cook for 1–2 minutes.

**3** Stir in half a ladleful of the hot liquid. Stir constantly until the liquid has been absorbed. Add another half ladleful of the liquid, and stir until it has also been absorbed. Continue stirring and adding the liquid, a little at a time, for about 10 minutes.

## COOK'S TIP

Parmesan cheese is ideal for cooking because it does not become stringy or rubbery when heated. It can be grated over many hot dishes, such as pasta and risotto, as well as added to cold salads. There are two basic types of Parmesan cheeses – Parmigiano Reggiano and Grana Padano – but the former is superior in quality.

**4** Add the remaining asparagus sections, and continue cooking, stirring and adding the liquid until the rice is *al dente*. Total cooking time will be about 30 minutes. If you run out of stock, use hot water, but do not worry if the rice is ready before all the stock has been added. Remove the pan from the heat and stir in the remaining butter and the Parmesan. Add a little black pepper and salt to taste. Serve at once.

# Risotto-stuffed Aubergines with Spicy Tomato Sauce

Aubergines are a challenge to the creative cook and allow for some unusual recipe ideas. Here, they are stuffed and baked with a cheese and pine nut topping.

## COOK'S TIP
If the aubergine shells do not stand level, cut a thin slice from the base. When browning the filled shells, use crumpled foil to support them.

### Serves 4

INGREDIENTS
4 small aubergines
105 ml/7 tbsp olive oil
1 small onion, chopped
175 g/6 oz/scant 1 cup risotto rice
750 ml/1¼ pints/3 cups hot
    vegetable stock
15 ml/1 tbsp white wine vinegar
25 g/1 oz/⅓ cup freshly grated
    Parmesan cheese
15 g/½ oz/2 tbsp pine nuts
8 fresh basil sprigs, to garnish

FOR THE TOMATO SAUCE
300 ml/½ pint/1¼ cups thick passata
    or tomato purée
5 ml/1 tsp mild curry paste
pinch of salt

*aubergines*

*wine vinegar*

*onion*   *vegetable stock*

*risotto rice*

*olive oil*

*Parmesan cheese*

*curry paste*   *passata*   *pine nuts*

**1** Preheat the oven to 200°C/400°F/Gas 6. Cut the aubergines in half lengthways and take out their flesh with a small knife. Brush the shells with 30 ml/2 tbsp of the oil, place on a baking sheet and bake for 6–8 minutes.

**2** Chop the reserved aubergine flesh. Heat the remainder of the olive oil in a medium saucepan. Add the aubergine flesh and the onion and cook over a gentle heat for about 3–4 minutes until just soft.

**3** Add the rice, stir in the stock and leave to simmer uncovered for a further 15 minutes. Stir in the vinegar.

**4** Increase the oven temperature to 230°C/450°F/Gas 8. Spoon the rice into the aubergine skins, top with the cheese and pine nuts, return to the oven and brown for 5 minutes.

**5** To make the sauce, mix the passata or tomato purée with the curry paste in a small pan. Heat through and add salt to taste.

**6** Spoon the sauce on to four large serving plates and position two stuffed aubergine halves on each. Garnish with basil sprigs.

# Leek, Mushroom and Lemon Risotto

A delicious risotto, packed full of flavour makes a marvellous treat for friends or family.

## Serves 4

INGREDIENTS
225 g/8 oz trimmed leeks
225 g/8 oz/2–3 cups brown cap
   mushrooms
30 ml/2 tbsp olive oil
3 garlic cloves, crushed
75 g/3 oz/6 tbsp butter
1 large onion, roughly chopped
350 g/12 oz/1³⁄₄ cups risotto rice
1.2 litres/2 pints/5 cups simmering
   vegetable stock
grated rind of 1 lemon
45 ml/3 tbsp lemon juice
50 g/2 oz/²⁄₃ cup freshly grated
   Parmesan cheese
60 ml/4 tbsp mixed chopped fresh
   chives and flat leaf parsley
salt and freshly ground black pepper
lemon wedges, to serve

leeks

olive oil

mushrooms

lemon   butter

risotto rice

Parmesan cheese

onion

garlic   vegetable stock

parsley   chives

**1** Wash the leeks well. Slice them in half lengthways and chop them roughly. Wipe the mushrooms with kitchen paper and chop them roughly.

**2** Heat the oil in a large saucepan and cook the garlic for 1 minute. Add the leeks, mushrooms and plenty of seasoning and cook over a medium heat for about 10 minutes, or until softened and browned. Remove from the pan and set aside.

**3** Add 25 g/1 oz of the butter to the pan. As soon as it has melted, add the onion and cook over a medium heat for 5 minutes until softened and golden.

**4** Stir in the rice and cook for about 1 minute until the grains begin to look translucent and are coated in the fat. Add a ladleful of stock to the pan and cook gently, stirring occasionally, until the liquid has been absorbed.

**5** Continue to add stock, a ladleful at a time, until all the stock has been absorbed. This should take about 25–30 minutes. The risotto will turn thick and creamy and the rice should be tender but not sticky.

**6** Just before serving, stir in the leeks, mushrooms, remaining butter, grated lemon rind and juice. Add half the grated Parmesan and herbs. Adjust the seasoning and serve, sprinkled with the remaining Parmesan, herbs and lemon wedges. Garnish with parsley, if you like.

# Shellfish Risotto with Mixed Mushrooms

The combination of shellfish and mushrooms in this creamy risotto is exquisite. Serve with chunks of hot ciabatta, if you like.

## Serves 4

INGREDIENTS
225 g/8 oz live mussels
225 g/8 oz Venus or carpet shell clams
45 ml/3 tbsp olive oil
1 onion, chopped
225 g/8 oz/2–3 cups assorted wild and cultivated mushrooms, trimmed and sliced
450 g/1 lb/2¼ cups risotto rice
1.2 litres/2 pints/5 cups hot chicken or vegetable stock
150 ml/¼ pint/⅔ cup white wine
115 g/4 oz cooked prawns, deveined, heads and tails removed
1 squid, cleaned, trimmed and sliced
3 drops truffle oil (optional)
75 ml/5 tbsp chopped fresh parsley and chervil
celery salt and cayenne pepper

olive oil
mushrooms
white wine
risotto rice
stock
onion
parsley
prawns
mussels
clams
truffle oil
squid

**1** Scrub the mussels and clams clean and tap them with a knife. If any shells do not close, discard them. Put aside. Heat the oil in a large saucepan and fry the onion for 6–8 minutes until soft but not browned.

**2** Add the mushrooms and allow them to soften, until their juices begin to run. Stir in the rice and heat through.

## COOK'S TIP

Use a mixture of mushrooms, such as ceps, bay boletus, chanterelles, chicken of the woods, saffron milk-caps, horn of plenty, wood blewits, oyster, St George's, Caesar's and truffles. Wash all mushrooms carefully, particularly wild ones. It is worth noting that chicken of the woods mushrooms may need blanching in boiling salted water for 2–3 minutes before cooking, to remove their slight bitter taste. Also, use truffles sparingly, as they have a strong flavour.

**3** Pour in the stock and wine. Add the prawns, mussels, clams and squid, stir gently and simmer for 15 minutes. If any of the mussels and clams do not open after cooking, discard them.

**4** Remove from the heat. Add the truffle oil if using, and stir in the herbs. Cover tightly and leave to stand for 5–10 minutes to allow all the flavours to blend. Season to taste with celery salt and a pinch of cayenne pepper and serve immediately.

# Salmon Risotto with Cucumber and Tarragon

Arborio or carnaroli rices are ideal for this simple and delicious risotto. Fresh tarragon and cucumber combine well in this recipe to bring out the flavour of the salmon, making a particularly delicate and fragrant dish.

### *Serves 4*

INGREDIENTS

25 g/1 oz/2 tbsp butter

1 small bunch of spring onions, white parts only, chopped

1/2 cucumber, peeled, seeded and chopped

400 g/14 oz/2 cups risotto rice

900 ml/1 1/2 pints/3 3/4 cups chicken or fish stock

150 ml/1/4 pint/2/3 cup dry white wine

450 g/1 lb salmon fillet, skinned and diced

45 ml/3 tbsp chopped fresh tarragon

**1** Heat the butter in a large saucepan and add the spring onions and cucumber. Cook for 2–3 minutes without colouring.

*butter*  *spring onions*

*stock*  *cucumber*

*salmon fillet*

*white wine*

*tarragon*

*risotto rice*

## VARIATION

Smoked salmon can be used instead of fresh. Buy offcuts, which are cheaper than slices, and cut them into bite-size pieces. Add right at the end, just before the standing time.

**2** Add the rice, stock and wine, return to the boil and simmer uncovered for 10 minutes, stirring occasionally.

**3** Stir in the diced salmon and tarragon. Continue cooking for a further 5 minutes, then switch off the heat. Cover and leave to stand for 5 minutes before serving.

# Risotto with Chicken

A classic combination of chicken and rice, cooked with Parma ham, white wine and Parmesan.

### Serves 4

INGREDIENTS

30 ml/2 tbsp olive oil
225 g/8 oz skinless, boneless chicken breast, cut into 2.5 cm/1 in cubes
1 onion, finely chopped
1 garlic clove, finely chopped
1.5 ml/¼ tsp saffron strands
50 g/2 oz Parma ham, cut into thin strips
450 g/1 lb/2¼ cups risotto rice
120 ml/4 fl oz/½ cup dry white wine
1.75 litres/3 pints/7½ cups simmering chicken stock
25 g/1 oz/2 tbsp butter (optional)
25 g/1 oz/⅓ cup freshly grated Parmesan cheese, plus more to serve
salt and freshly ground black pepper
flat leaf parsley, to garnish

olive oil · onion · garlic · saffron · chicken · risotto rice · stock · white wine · Parma ham · butter · Parmesan cheese · parsley

**1** Heat the oil in a wide heavy-based pan over moderately high heat. Add the chicken cubes and cook, stirring, until they start to turn white.

**2** Reduce the heat to low and add the onion, garlic, saffron and Parma ham. Cook, stirring, until the onion is soft. Stir in the rice. Sauté for 1–2 minutes, stirring constantly.

**3** Add the wine and bring to the boil. Simmer gently until almost all the wine has been absorbed. Add the simmering stock, a ladleful at a time, until absorbed and cook until the rice is just tender and the risotto is creamy.

**4** Add the butter, if using, and the Parmesan cheese and stir in well. Season with salt and pepper to taste. Serve the risotto hot, sprinkled with a little more Parmesan, and garnish with parsley.

# Risotto with Smoky Bacon and Tomato

A classic risotto, with plenty of onions, smoked bacon and sun-dried tomatoes. You'll want to keep going back for more!

## Serves 4

INGREDIENTS

8 sun-dried tomatoes in olive oil
275 g/10 oz good-quality rindless smoked back bacon
75 g/3 oz/6 tbsp butter
450 g/1 lb onions, roughly chopped
2 garlic cloves, crushed
350 g/12 oz/1¾ cups risotto rice
300 ml/½ pint/1¼ cups dry white wine
900 ml/1½ pints/3¾ cups simmering vegetable stock
50 g/2 oz/⅔ cup freshly grated Parmesan cheese
45 ml/3 tbsp mixed chopped fresh chives and flat leaf parsley
salt and freshly ground black pepper
flat leaf parsley sprigs, to garnish
lemon wedges, to serve

flat leaf parsley

smoked bacon

chives

vegetable stock

butter

garlic

Parmesan cheese

sun-dried tomatoes

white wine

risotto rice

onions

lemon

**1** Drain the sun-dried tomatoes and reserve 15 ml/1 tbsp of the oil. Roughly chop the tomatoes and set aside. Cut the bacon into 2.5 cm/1 in strips.

**2** Heat the reserved sun-dried tomato oil in a large saucepan. Fry the bacon until well cooked and golden. Remove with a slotted spoon and drain on kitchen paper.

**3** Add 25 g/1 oz/2 tbsp of the butter to the pan. When it melts add the onions and garlic. Cook over a medium heat for 10 minutes, until softened and golden brown.

**4** Stir in the rice. Cook for 1 minute until turning translucent. Stir the wine into the simmering stock. Add a ladleful to the rice and cook gently until absorbed.

**5** Stir in another ladleful of the stock and wine mixture and allow it to be absorbed again. Repeat this process until all the liquid is used up. This should take 25–30 minutes. The risotto will turn thick and creamy, and the rice should be tender but not sticky.

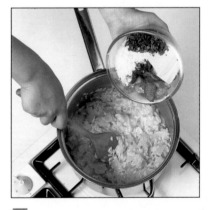

**6** Just before serving, stir in the bacon, sun-dried tomatoes, half the Parmesan and herbs, and the remaining butter. Adjust the seasoning (remember that the bacon may be quite salty) and serve sprinkled with the remaining Parmesan and herbs. Garnish with parsley and serve with lemon wedges.

# SIDE DISHES

## Egg Fried Rice

This is perhaps one of the most famous of side dishes. Use rice with a fairly firm texture. Ideally, the rice should be soaked in water for a short time before cooking.

### Serves 4

INGREDIENTS

3 eggs
5 ml/1 tsp salt
2 spring onions, finely chopped
30–45 ml/2–3 tbsp oil
175 g/6 oz/scant 1 cup long grain rice, cooked and cooled
115 g/4 oz/1 cup peas, thawed if frozen

*spring onions*

*peas*

*long grain rice*   *oil*   *eggs*   *salt*

**1** In a bowl, lightly beat the eggs with a pinch of the salt and a few pieces of the chopped spring onions. Heat a wok and when it is hot add some oil. When the oil is hot add the eggs and lightly scramble them.

**2** Add the cooked rice and stir to make sure that each grain of rice stays separate. Add the remaining salt, spring onions and the peas. Mix well and stir-fry for a few minutes, until the rice is piping hot. Serve immediately.

## Coconut Rice

This side dish is popular in Thailand, where jasmine rice is commonly eaten and coconut is used in many recipes. Rich and delicious, this tastes great with a tangy papaya salad.

### Serves 4–6

INGREDIENTS

450 g/1 lb/2¼ cups jasmine rice
475 ml/16 fl oz/2 cups coconut milk
2.5 ml/½ tsp salt
30 ml/2 tbsp sugar
fresh shredded coconut, to garnish (optional)

*fresh coconut*   *salt*   *jasmine rice*

*sugar*   *coconut milk*

**1** Wash the rice in several changes of cold water until it runs clear. Place the coconut milk, salt and sugar in a heavy-bottomed saucepan. Add 250 ml/8 fl oz/1 cup water and stir in the rice. Cover and bring to the boil. Reduce the heat and simmer for 15–20 minutes or until the rice is *al dente*.

**2** Turn off the heat, cover and allow the rice to rest in the saucepan for a further 5–10 minutes. Fluff up the rice with chopsticks before serving. Garnish with shredded coconut, if you like.

# Special Fried Rice

Special Fried Rice is a very popular rice recipe in China. As it contains prawns and ham, it can almost make a meal in itself.

## Serves 4

INGREDIENTS

50 g/2 oz cooked prawns, peeled
50 g/2 oz cooked ham
3 eggs
5 ml/1 tsp salt
2 spring onions, finely chopped, plus
   extra to garnish
60 ml/4 tbsp oil
115 g/4 oz/1 cup peas, thawed if
   frozen
15 ml/1 tbsp light soy sauce
15 ml/1 tbsp Chinese rice wine or
   dry sherry
175 g/6 oz/scant 1 cup long grain
   rice, cooked

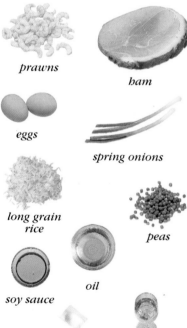

*prawns*

*ham*

*eggs*

*spring onions*

*long grain rice*

*peas*

*soy sauce*

*oil*

*salt*

*sherry*

**1** Pat the cooked prawns dry with kitchen paper, making sure no moisture remains. Cut the ham into small dice about the same size as the peas.

**2** In a bowl, lightly beat the eggs with a pinch of the salt and a few pieces of the chopped spring onions, using chopsticks or a fork.

## COOK'S TIP
Chinese rice wine can be found in Chinese supermarkets and ethnic food shops.

**3** Heat the wok, add about half of the oil and when it is hot, stir-fry the peas, prawns and ham for about 1 minute. Add the soy sauce and rice wine or sherry. Transfer the mixture to a dish and keep hot.

**4** Heat the remaining oil in the wok and scramble the eggs lightly. Add the rice and stir to separate the grains. Add the remaining salt and spring onions and the prawn mixture. Stir well and heat until the rice is piping hot. Garnish with chopped spring onions.

# Long Grain and Wild Rice Ring

This American-style side dish combines two types of rice with currants and onion, to give an unusual texture and delicious flavour.

## Serves 8

INGREDIENTS

30 ml/2 tbsp corn oil, plus extra for greasing mould
1 large onion, chopped
400 g/14 oz/2 cups mixed long grain and wild rice
1.2 litres/2 pints/5 cups chicken stock
50 g/2 oz/¹/₃ cup currants
salt
6 spring onions, cut diagonally into 5 mm/¹/₄ in pieces
fresh parsley sprigs, to garnish

*corn oil*

*spring onions*

*onion*

*chicken stock*

*parsley*

*mixed long grain and wild rice*

*currants*

**1** Lightly oil a 1.75 litre/3 pint/7¹/₂ cup ring mould. Set aside. Heat the oil in a large saucepan. Add the onion and cook for 5 minutes, or until softened.

**2** Add the rice to the pan and stir well to coat the rice with the oil.

**3** Stir in the chicken stock and bring to the boil. Reduce the heat to low. Stir the currants into the rice mixture. Add salt to taste. Cover and simmer until the rice is tender and the stock has been absorbed, about 35 minutes. Drain the rice if necessary and transfer it to a mixing bowl. Stir in the spring onions.

**4** Pack the rice mixture into the prepared mould. Turn it on to a warmed serving platter. Place parsley sprigs in the centre of the ring before serving.

## COOK'S TIP

Wild rice needs quite a lengthy cooking time and so you will need a particularly large amount of water for boiling it in. It will, however, need a shorter cooking time if mixed with a long grain rice. Wild rice is ready when the grains have begun to burst open, releasing their nutty aroma.

# Okra Fried Rice

If you like hot food, you'll love this spicy vegetable Caribbean speciality.

## Serves 3-4

INGREDIENTS

150 g/5 oz okra
30 ml/2 tbsp oil
15 g/¹/₂ oz/1 tbsp butter or margarine
1 garlic clove, crushed
¹/₂ red onion, finely chopped
30 ml/2 tbsp diced green and red peppers
2.5 ml/¹/₂ tsp dried thyme
2 green chillies, finely chopped
2.5 ml/¹/₂ tsp five-spice powder
¹/₂ vegetable stock cube
30 ml/2 tbsp soy sauce
15 ml/1 tbsp chopped fresh coriander
175 g/6 oz/scant 1 cup long grain rice, cooked
freshly ground black pepper
fresh coriander sprigs, to garnish

*oil*

*butter*

*red onion*

*green and red peppers*

*stock cube*

*garlic*

*green chillies*

*thyme*

*okra*

*five-spice powder*

*soy sauce*

*coriander*

*long grain rice*

**1** Wash and dry the okra, remove the tops and tails and slice thinly and diagonally. Set aside until needed.

**2** Heat the oil and butter or margarine in a frying pan or wok, add the garlic and onion and cook over a moderate heat for 5 minutes until soft. Add the sliced okra and sauté gently for 6–7 minutes.

**3** Add the green and red peppers, thyme, chillies and five-spice powder and cook for 3 minutes.

**4** Crumble in the stock cube, add the soy sauce, coriander and rice and toss over the heat until the rice is piping hot. Add some freshly ground pepper. Serve, garnished with the coriander sprigs.

# Pilau Rice Flavoured with Whole Spices

This fragrant rice dish will make a perfect accompaniment to any Indian meal.

## Serves 4-6

INGREDIENTS
generous pinch of saffron strands
600 ml/1 pint/2½ cups hot chicken
    stock
50 g/2 oz/¼ cup butter
1 onion, chopped
1 garlic clove, crushed
½ cinnamon stick
6 green cardamoms
1 bay leaf
250 g/9 oz/1⅓ cup basmati rice,
    rinsed and drained
50 g/2 oz/⅓ cup sultanas
15 ml/1 tbsp oil
50 g/2 oz/½ cup cashew nuts

**1** Add the saffron strands to the hot stock and set aside. Heat the butter in a large saucepan and fry the onion and garlic for 5 minutes. Stir in the cinnamon stick, cardamoms and bay leaf and cook for 2 minutes.

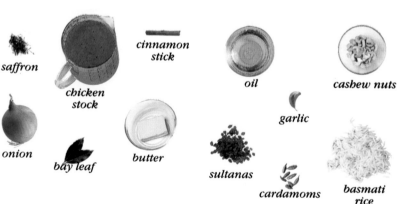

saffron

chicken
stock

cinnamon
stick

oil

cashew nuts

garlic

onion

bay leaf

butter

sultanas

cardamoms

basmati
rice

**2** Add the rice and cook, stirring, for 2 minutes more. Pour in the stock and saffron mixture and add the sultanas. Bring to the boil, stir, then lower the heat. Cover the pan and leave to cook gently for about 15 minutes or until the rice is tender and all the liquid has been absorbed.

**3** Meanwhile, heat the oil in a wok or frying pan and fry the cashew nuts until browned. Drain on kitchen paper. Scatter over the rice and serve.

## VARIATION

You can add a mixture of nuts to this recipe, if you like, such as almonds, peanuts or hazelnuts. Some nuts may be bought complete with their brown, papery skins, which should be removed before use. The flavour of all nuts is improved by toasting.

## COOK'S TIP

Remember to keep all spices stored in separate airtight containers. This helps them to retain their flavour as well as preventing their aromas from spreading to other ingredients in your store cupboard.

# Mexican-style Rice

This side dish is the perfect accompaniment for chicken fajitas or flour tortillas. It is garnished with a stunning but dangerous display of flowers made from red chillies.

## Serves 6

INGREDIENTS
350 g/12 oz/1¾ cups long grain rice
1 onion, chopped
2 garlic cloves, chopped
450 g/1 lb tomatoes, peeled, seeded and coarsely chopped
60 ml/4 tbsp corn or peanut oil
900 ml/1½ pints/3¾ cups chicken stock
175 g/6 oz/1½ cups peas, thawed if frozen
salt and freshly ground black pepper
fresh coriander sprigs and 4–6 red chilli flowers, to garnish

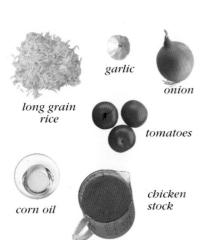

long grain rice

garlic

onion

tomatoes

corn oil

chicken stock

coriander

red chillies

peas

**1** Soak the rice in a bowl of hot water for 15 minutes. Drain, rinse well under cold running water, drain again and set aside. Combine the onion, garlic and tomatoes in a food processor and process to a purée.

**2** Heat the oil in a large frying pan. Add the drained rice and sauté until it becomes golden brown. Using a slotted spoon, to leave behind as much oil as possible, transfer the rice to a saucepan.

## COOK'S TIP
To make chilli flowers, it is a good idea to wear rubber gloves and avoid touching your face or eyes, as the essential oils will cause a painful reaction. Slice the red chillies from tip to stem end into four or five sections. Place in a bowl of iced water until they curl back to form flowers, then drain. Wash hands or gloves thoroughly.

**3** Reheat the oil remaining in the pan and cook the tomato, garlic and onion purée for 2–3 minutes. Tip it into the saucepan of rice and pour in the stock. Season to taste. Bring to the boil, reduce the heat to the lowest possible setting, cover the pan and cook for about 15–20 minutes until almost all the liquid has been absorbed.

**4** Stir the peas into the rice mixture and cook, without a lid, until all the liquid has been absorbed and the rice is tender. Stir the mixture from time to time. Transfer the rice to a serving dish and garnish with the drained chilli flowers and sprigs of coriander. Warn the diners that the chilli flowers are hot and should be approached with caution.

# Rice Flavoured with Saffron and Cardamom

This rice is delicately flavoured with three aromatic spices to create a superb side dish. Serve it as an accompaniment to your favourite Indian curry.

## Serves 6

INGREDIENTS
450 g/1 lb/2¼ cups basmati rice
3 green cardamoms
2 cloves
5 ml/1 tsp salt
2.5 ml/½ tsp crushed saffron strands
45 ml/3 tbsp milk

basmati rice · milk · cloves · saffron · salt · cardamom

**1** Wash the rice thoroughly, at least twice, drain and place in a saucepan with 750 ml/1¼ pints/3 cups of water.

**2** Toss the cardamoms and cloves into the saucepan along with the salt. Bring to the boil, cover, lower the heat and simmer for about 10 minutes. Meanwhile, place the saffron and milk in a small pan and warm.

## COOK'S TIP

Saffron, the world's most expensive spice, is made from the stamen of the *Crocus Sativus*. Two hundred thousand flowers are harvested by hand to obtain every 450 g/1 lb saffron, which explains its high value. It is appreciated for its delicate yet distinctive flavour and striking colour, and is added to special dishes in many cuisines, savoury as well as sweet.

**3** To see if the rice is fully cooked, use a slotted spoon to lift out a few grains and press the rice between your index finger and thumb. It should feel soft on the outside but still a little hard in the middle (*al dente*). Remove the pan from the heat and drain the rice through a sieve.

**4** Tip the rice and whole spices back into the pan and spoon the saffron milk over the top of the rice.

**5** Cover the pan with a tight-fitting lid and return to a medium heat for about 7–10 minutes. Remove the pan from the heat, leaving the lid on, and let the rice stand for a further 5 minutes before it is served.

# Tomato Rice

This vibrant rice dish owes its appeal as much to the bright colours of red onion, red pepper and cherry tomatoes as it does to their luscious, distinctive flavours.

## Serves 2

INGREDIENTS
115 g/4 oz/²⁄₃ cup basmati rice
30 ml/2 tbsp groundnut oil
1 small red onion, chopped
1 red pepper, seeded and chopped
225 g/8 oz cherry tomatoes, halved
2 eggs, beaten
salt and freshly ground black pepper
chopped fresh herbs, to garnish

*eggs*

*groundnut oil*

*red pepper*

*cherry tomatoes*

*red onion*

*mixed herbs*

*basmati rice*

## COOK'S TIP

Groundnut oil is made from peanuts and has a very distinctive taste. Use it carefully at first, until you become used to the flavour. If you use groundnut oil or any peanut product, always check that none of your guests is allergic to peanuts. Use corn oil instead, if you like.

**1** Wash the rice several times under cold running water. Drain well. Bring a large pan of water to the boil, add the rice and cook for 10–12 minutes.

**2** Meanwhile, heat the oil in a wok until very hot. Add the onion and red pepper and stir-fry for 2–3 minutes. Add the cherry tomatoes and stir-fry for a further 2 minutes. Pour in the beaten eggs all at once.

**3** Cook for 30 seconds without stirring, then stir to break up the eggs as they begin to set.

**4** Drain the cooked rice thoroughly, add to the wok and toss it over the heat with the vegetable and egg mixture for 3 minutes. Season to taste. Garnish with chopped herbs.

# Pigeon Peas Cook-up Rice

This Guyanese-style rice dish is made with the country's most commonly used peas. It is flavoured with creamed coconut, another popular West Indian ingredient.

### Serves 4-6

INGREDIENTS

25 g/1 oz/2 tbsp butter or margarine
1 onion, chopped
1 garlic clove, crushed
25 g/1 oz/2 tbsp chopped spring onions
1 large carrot, diced
175 g/6 oz/about 1 cup pigeon peas
1 fresh thyme sprig or 5 ml/1 tsp dried thyme
1 cinnamon stick
600 ml/1 pint/2½ cups vegetable stock
65 g/2½ oz/4 tbsp creamed coconut
1 red chilli, chopped
450 g/1 lb/2¼ cups long grain rice
salt and freshly ground black pepper

butter

onion

spring onion

cinnamon

garlic

carrot

chilli

vegetable stock

long grain rice

creamed coconut

thyme

## COOK'S TIP

Pigeon peas are also known as gunga peas. The fresh peas can be difficult to obtain, but you will find them in specialist shops. The frozen peas are green and the canned variety are brown. Drain the salted water from canned peas and rinse before using them in this recipe.

**1** Melt the butter or margarine in a large heavy saucepan, add the chopped onion and crushed garlic and sauté over a medium heat for about 5 minutes, stirring occasionally.

**2** Add the spring onions, carrot, pigeon peas, thyme, cinnamon, stock, creamed coconut, chilli and seasoning. Bring to the boil.

**3** Reduce the heat and then stir in the rice. Cover and simmer over a low heat for about 10–15 minutes, or until all the liquid has been absorbed and the rice is tender. Stir with a fork to fluff up the rice before serving.

# Rice Cakes with Cream and Mixed Mushrooms

Serve with rich meat dishes such as beef stroganoff or goulash, or as part of a vegetarian supper menu.

*Serves 4*

INGREDIENTS

165 g/5¹/₂ oz/³/₄ cup long grain rice
1 egg
15 ml/1 tbsp plain flour
60 ml/4 tbsp freshly grated Parmesan, Fontina or Pecorino cheese
50 g/2 oz/¹/₄ cup unsalted butter, plus extra for frying rice cakes
1 small onion, chopped
175 g/6 oz/1¹/₂-2 cups assorted wild and cultivated mushrooms, trimmed and sliced
1 fresh thyme sprig
30 ml/2 tbsp Madeira or sherry
150 ml/¹/₄ pint/²/₃ cup soured cream or crème fraîche
salt and freshly ground black pepper
paprika for dusting (optional)

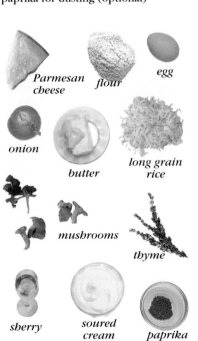

*Parmesan cheese*  *flour*  *egg*

*onion*  *butter*  *long grain rice*

*mushrooms*  *thyme*

*sherry*  *soured cream*  *paprika*

**1** Bring a saucepan of water to the boil. Add the rice and cook for about 12 minutes. Rinse, drain and cool.

**2** Beat the egg, flour and cheese together with a fork, then stir in the cold cooked rice. Mix well and set aside. Melt half the butter and fry the onion until soft but not browned. Add the mushrooms and thyme and cook until the juices run. Add the Madeira or sherry. Increase the heat to reduce the juices and concentrate the flavour. Season to taste, transfer to a bowl, cover and keep hot.

**3** Using a dessert spoon, shape the rice mixture into cakes. Melt a knob of butter in a frying pan and fry the rice cakes in batches for 1 minute on each side. Add more butter as needed. Keep the fried rice cakes hot.

**4** When all the rice cakes are cooked, arrange on four warmed plates, top with soured cream or crème fraîche and add a spoonful of mushrooms. Dust with paprika, if using. Serve with a selection of cooked vegetables, if you like.

## COOK'S TIP

Although the recipe specifies Parmesan, Fontina or Pecorino, you could use mature Cheddar cheese or even a hard goat's cheese.

# Rice and Vegetable Stir-fry

If you have some left-over cooked rice and a few vegetables to spare, then you've got the basis for this quick and tasty side dish.

*Serves 4*

INGREDIENTS
½ cucumber
1 small red or yellow pepper
2 carrots
45 ml/3 tbsp sunflower or groundnut oil
2 spring onions, sliced
1 garlic clove, crushed
¼ small green cabbage, shredded
75 g/3 oz/scant ½ cup cup long grain rice, cooked
30 ml/2 tbsp light soy sauce
15 ml/1 tbsp sesame oil
fresh parsley or coriander, chopped (optional)
115 g/4 oz/1 cup unsalted cashew nuts, almonds or peanuts
salt and freshly ground black pepper

*cucumber*

*spring onions*

*carrots*

*garlic*

*pepper*

*green cabbage*

*soy sauce*

*long grain rice*

*sunflower oil*

*parsley*

*sesame oil*

*cashew nuts*

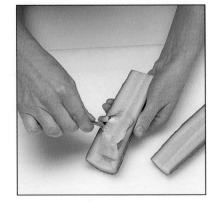

**1** Halve the cucumber lengthways and scoop out the seeds with a teaspoon. Slice the flesh diagonally. Set aside.

**2** Cut the red or yellow pepper in half and remove the core and seeds. Slice the pepper thinly.

**3** Peel the carrots and cut in thin slices. Heat the oil in a wok or large frying pan and stir-fry the sliced spring onions, garlic, carrots and pepper for 3 minutes until the vegetables are crisp but still tender.

**4** Add the cabbage and cucumber and fry for another minute or two until the leaves begin to wilt. Mix in the rice, soy sauce, sesame oil and seasoning. Reheat the mixture thoroughly, stirring and tossing all the time. Add the herbs, if using, and nuts. Check the seasoning and adjust if necessary. Serve piping hot.

# Sticky Rice with Tropical Fruit Topping

A popular dessert. Mangoes, with their delicate fragrance, sweet and sour flavour and velvety flesh, blend especially well with coconut sticky rice. You need to start preparing this dish the day before.

*Serves 4*

INGREDIENTS
115 g/4 oz/²/₃ cup glutinous (sticky) rice
175 ml/6 fl oz/³/₄ cup thick coconut milk
45 ml/3 tbsp sugar
pinch of salt
2 ripe mangoes
strips of lime rind, to decorate

*glutinous rice*

*coconut milk*

*sugar*

*mangoes*

*lime*

**1** Rinse the glutinous rice thoroughly in several changes of cold water, then leave to soak overnight in a bowl of fresh, cold water. Drain and spread the rice in an even layer in a steamer lined with cheesecloth. Cover and steam for about 20 minutes or until the grains of rice are tender.

**2** Meanwhile, reserve 45 ml/3 tbsp of the top of the coconut milk and combine the rest with the sugar and salt in a saucepan. Bring to the boil, stirring until the sugar dissolves, then pour into a bowl and leave to cool a little. Turn the rice into a bowl and pour over the coconut mixture. Stir, then leave for about 10–15 minutes.

**3** Peel the mangoes and cut the flesh into slices. Place on top of the rice and drizzle over the reserved coconut milk. Decorate with strips of lime rind.

## VARIATION
If mangoes are not available, top the sticky rice pudding with a compote, made by poaching ready-to-eat dried apricots in water to cover for about 15 minutes.

# Caramel Rice

Indulge in this version of the classic sweet rice dish, which is particularly delicious when served with fresh fruit.

## *Serves 4*

INGREDIENTS
50 g/2 oz/$^1$/₃ cup short grain pudding rice
75 ml/5 tbsp demerara sugar
pinch of salt
400 g/14 oz can evaporated milk made up to 600 ml/1 pint/2$^1$/₂ cups with water
knob of butter
1 small fresh pineapple
2 crisp eating apples
10 ml/2 tsp lemon juice

*short grain rice*

*lemon*

*pineapple*

*eating apples*

*evaporated milk*

*demerara sugar*

*butter*

**1** Preheat the oven to 150°C/300°F/ Gas 2. Put the rice in a sieve and wash under running cold water. Drain well and put into a lightly greased soufflé dish. Add 30 ml/2 tbsp of the sugar and the salt to the dish. Pour on the diluted evaporated milk and stir gently. Dot the surface of the rice with butter. Bake for 2 hours in the oven, then leave to cool for about 30 minutes.

## COOK'S TIP
Rice pudding is a popular dessert in many different countries, and so the possibilities for making different variations are endless. You can try sprinkling grated nutmeg on the top instead of sugar or decorate it with chopped almonds, pistachios and ground cinnamon. Rice pudding is also delicious chilled.

**2** Meanwhile, peel, core and slice the pineapple and apples, then cut the pineapple into chunks. Toss the fruit in the lemon juice and set aside.

**3** Preheat the grill and sprinkle the remaining sugar over the rice pudding. Grill for 5 minutes until the sugar has caramelized. Leave the rice to stand for 5 minutes to allow the caramel to harden, then serve with the fresh fruit.

# Fragrant Rice Dessert with Mango Purée

Nuts, dried fruit, cardamom and rosewater make this Indian-style rice pudding a real treat.

*Serves 6*

INGREDIENTS
2 ripe mangoes
50 g/2 oz/scant $^1$/$_3$ cup basmati rice
1.5 litres/2$^1$/$_2$ pints/6$^1$/$_4$ cups milk
50 g/2 oz/$^1$/$_4$ cup demerara sugar
50 g/2 oz/$^1$/$_3$ cup sultanas
5 ml/1 tsp rosewater
5 green cardamoms
45 ml/3 tbsp orange juice
45 ml/3 tbsp flaked almonds, toasted
45 ml/3 tbsp pistachio nuts, chopped

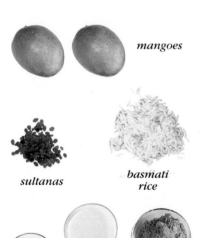

*mangoes*

*sultanas*  *basmati rice*

*orange juice*  *milk*  *demerara sugar*

*cardamom*  *flaked almonds*  *pistachio nuts*

**1** Using a sharp knife, peel, slice and stone the mangoes.

**2** Preheat the oven to 150°C/300°F/ Gas 2. Put the basmati rice in an ovenproof dish. Bring the milk to the boil in a saucepan, then pour it over the rice. Bake uncovered for 2 hours until the rice has become soft and mushy.

**3** Remove the dish from the oven and stir in the demerara sugar and sultanas, with half the rosewater. Crush the cardamom pods, extract the seeds and stir them into the rice mixture. Allow to cool.

**4** Place the mango flesh in a blender or food processor. Add the orange juice and remaining rosewater. Blend until smooth. Divide the mango purée among six individual glass serving dishes. Spoon the rice pudding mixture evenly over the top. Leave to chill thoroughly in the fridge. When ready to serve, scatter the toasted almonds and chopped pistachio nuts over the top of each pudding.

## VARIATION

Make this nutritious dessert an even healthier option by decorating with slices of fruit instead of nuts.

# Mexican Rice Pudding

Here is another delicious version of the classic rice dessert. This Mexican recipe – *Arroz con Leche* – is light and attractive and combines many tantalizing flavours. It is surprisingly easy to make.

*Serves 4*

INGREDIENTS

75 g/3 oz/¹⁄₂ cup raisins
90 g/3¹⁄₂ oz/¹⁄₂ cup short grain rice
2.5 cm/1 in strip of pared lime or lemon rind
475 ml/16 fl oz/2 cups milk
225 g/8 oz/1 cup granulated sugar
1.5 ml/¹⁄₄ tsp salt
2.5 cm/1 in piece of cinnamon stick
2 egg yolks, well beaten
15 g/¹⁄₂ oz/1 tbsp unsalted butter, cubed
toasted flaked almonds to decorate
segments of fresh peeled oranges, to serve

*raisins*

*short grain rice*

*milk*

*cinnamon*

*lime*

*eggs*

*oranges*

*sugar*

*butter*

*flaked almonds*

**1** Soak the raisins in warm water to cover until plump. Place the rice in a saucepan with 250 ml/8 fl oz/1 cup water and the citrus rind. Bring slowly to the boil, then cover and simmer for 20 minutes until the water is absorbed.

**2** Remove the rind from the rice and discard it. Add the milk, sugar, salt and cinnamon and cook, stirring, over a very low heat until all the milk has been absorbed. Do not cover the pan.

**3** Discard the cinnamon stick. Beat in the egg yolks. Drain the raisins well and stir them into the rice. Add the cubed butter and stir until it has melted and the pudding is rich and creamy. Cook the pudding for a few minutes longer.

**4** Scrape the rice into a dish and cool. Decorate with the almonds and serve with the orange segments.

95

# Rice Pudding with Mixed Berry Sauce

An irresistible combination of creamy rice with refreshing summer fruits that gives a new meaning to the phrase "comfort food".

## Serves 6

INGREDIENTS
400 g/14 oz/2 cups short grain rice
300 ml/¹/₂ pint/1¹/₄ cups milk
pinch of salt
115 g/4 oz/²/₃ cup soft light brown
  sugar
5 ml/1 tsp vanilla essence
2 eggs, beaten
grated rind of 1 lemon
5 ml/1 tsp fresh lemon juice
25 g/1 oz/2 tbsp butter or margarine
strawberry leaves, to decorate
  (optional)

FOR THE SAUCE
175 g/6 oz/1¹/₄ cups strawberries,
  hulled and quartered
225 g/8 oz/1¹/₂ cups raspberries
115 g/4 oz/¹/₂ cup granulated sugar
grated rind of 1 lemon

short grain rice

vanilla essence

eggs

lemon

milk

light brown sugar

butter

raspberries

strawberries

sugar

**1** Preheat the oven to 160°C/325°F/ Gas 3. Grease a 1 litre/1³/₄ pint/4 cup baking dish. Bring a saucepan of water to the boil. Add the rice and boil for 5 minutes. Drain. Transfer the rice to the prepared baking dish.

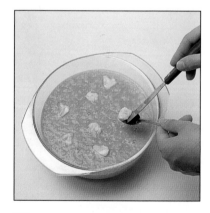

**2** In a bowl, combine the milk, salt, brown sugar, vanilla, eggs, and lemon rind and juice. Pour this mixture over the rice and stir well. Dot the surface of the rice mixture with the butter or margarine. Bake for about 50 minutes, until the rice is cooked and creamy.

**3** Meanwhile, make the sauce. Mix the berries and granulated sugar in a small saucepan. Stir over a low heat until the sugar has dissolved completely and the fruit is becoming pulpy. Transfer to a bowl and stir in the lemon rind. Chill the sauce until required.

**4** Remove the rice pudding from the oven. Allow to cool completely, and serve with the berry sauce. Decorate with strawberry leaves, if you like.

# Thai-style Dessert

Black glutinous rice, also known as black sticky rice, makes a tasty pudding. It tastes nutty, rather like wild rice.

*Serves 4-6*

INGREDIENTS

175 g/6 oz/scant 1 cup black glutinous (sticky) rice
30 ml/2 tbsp soft light brown sugar
475 ml/16 fl oz/2 cups coconut milk
3 eggs
30 ml/2 tbsp granulated sugar

*soft light brown sugar*

*coconut milk*

*eggs*

*black glutinous rice*

*granulated sugar*

**1** Combine the glutinous rice, brown sugar, half the coconut milk and 250 ml/8 fl oz/1 cup of water in a saucepan. Bring to the boil, then simmer for about 15–20 minutes or until the rice has absorbed most of the liquid, stirring from time to time. Preheat the oven to 150°C/300°F/Gas 2.

**3** Place the dish or ramekins in a baking tin. Pour in enough boiling water to come halfway up the sides of the dishes. Cover with foil and bake in the oven for about 35 minutes to 1 hour or until the custard is set. Serve warm or cold, whichever you prefer.

## VARIATION

Black glutinous rice is popular in South-east Asia for sweet dishes. Its character contributes to the delicious flavour of this dessert. Use white glutinous rice if the black grain is difficult to find.

**2** Transfer the rice into one large ovenproof dish or divide it among individual ramekins. Mix the eggs, remaining coconut milk and granulated sugar in a bowl. Strain and pour the mixture evenly over the rice mixture.

## COOK'S TIP

A pan of water in which dishes of delicate food are cooked, is known as a *bain marie*.

# noodles

Chinese noodles

**wheat noodles**

**egg noodles**

cellophane noodles

**rice noodles**

rice vermicelli

**Japanese noodles**

**gyoza wrappers**

Harusame noodles

Soba noodles

somen noodles

udon noodles

river rice noodles

spring roll wrappers

wonton wrappers

# INTRODUCING NOODLES

Noodles are loved the world over and are used in countless recipes. Thanks to Marco Polo, noodles have an undisputed place in western kitchens, but this section concentrates on the noodle dishes of Asia. China, Thailand, Japan and Indonesia, together with Vietnam, Burma and Malaysia, have their own traditional noodle dishes and many of these have become as popular in the west as they are in their own countries. Chow mein, Singapore Noodles, Thai Fried Noodles and Sukiyaki from Japan are now among our own favourites and are just a few of the many superb dishes featured in this section.

Unlike Italian pasta, which is produced almost exclusively from wheat, Asian noodles are also made from rice, pea starch and even from arrowroot, generally depending on the principal crop of the region. Wheat noodles are one of the staple foods of northern China, where wheat is the primary grain. These are made with or without egg and are sold in a huge variety of widths, from fine vermicelli strands to thick and broad ribbons. Rice noodles, characterized by their opaque, pale colour, also come in a range of widths, while cellophane noodles are thin and wiry, used for soups or adding to vegetable dishes.

In many cuisines, noodles play an important role in traditional festivities. In China they are a symbol of longevity, eaten at birthdays and weddings and as 'crossing of the threshold of the year' food. They are also a favourite snack food, sold on the street, tossed simply with flavoured oils, garlic or ginger or served with meat and vegetables. Noodles are the original fast food in the East, sold everywhere and for everyone at any time of the day. This section offers a selection of all types of noodle dishes, from soups and snacks to main meals for the family and special occasions.

# Types of Noodle

The range of Asian noodles is extensive, from fine and thin to coarse and thick, made of wheat flour (with or without egg), rice flour or vegetable starch, and available fresh or dried. They are amazingly versatile.

### Chinese noodles

Depending on the region and therefore on locally grown produce, Chinese noodles are made from one of three main ingredients – wheat flour, rice flour or mung beans. They come in a variety of shapes and thicknesses, often tied into bundles with raffia, or coiled into squares or oblongs. They are traditionally long, as this is believed to symbolize a long life.

Although most South East Asian countries produce their own noodles, Chinese-style noodles can be used for any of the speciality dishes from Malaysia, Indonesia and Thailand. Like pasta, most noodles are interchangeable, and if a certain type or thickness of noodle isn't available, a similar one can be used instead. The exception is cellophane noodles, which are used more as a vegetable to give texture to a dish, rather than as a staple.

### Wheat noodles

These come from northern China where wheat is the principal grain. Pure wheat noodles are often packaged like Italian spaghetti, in long thin sticks, or wound into nests.

### Egg noodles

Egg noodles are the most common and most versatile of all Chinese noodles. They are made from wheat with egg added, giving the characteristic yellow colour. Fresh egg noodles, such as those used for chow mein, are becoming increasingly available, not only in Chinese stores, but also in most large supermarkets. They are usually sold in thick coils and resemble balls of wool.

Dried egg noodles are normally coiled into compressed squares or oblongs. They come in a variety of thicknesses, from the thin, thread-like noodles, to broad, thick strips, and they can be ribbon-shaped or rounded.

Fresh noodles, like fresh pasta, have a better flavour and texture, but for cooking times check the packet instructions, as these will depend on their thickness. Dried noodles are best soaked briefly in warm water to untangle before adding to your dish.

### Cellophane, Mung bean or Pea starch noodles

These are made from ground mung beans and are also known as bean thread, transparent or glass noodles. They are thin and wiry and sold in bundles tied with a thread, but unlike rice vermicelli, they are translucent and are not brittle, and can only be broken up using scissors.

The dried noodles need to be soaked before cooking, and then can be used in soups and other dishes with plenty of sauce or stock, as they absorb four times their weight in liquid.

In a continent where texture is as important as flavour, these slippery-textured noodles are very popular, and while they have little or no flavour of their own, they will take on the flavours of other ingredients.

### Rice noodles

Made from ground rice, these come from southern parts of China, where rice is the staple crop. They range in thickness from very thin to wide ribbons and sheets. Dried ribbon rice noodles are usually sold tied together in bundles or come coiled into square packages.

### Rice vermicelli

Made from rice flour, these noodles are very thin, white and brittle, and are sold in large bundles, often tied with cotton or raffia. They should be soaked briefly and will then cook almost instantly in hot liquid. In their dried form they can be deep-fried for crispy noodles – don't soak them first.

*plain flour noodles*

*fresh medium egg noodles*

*rice vermicelli*

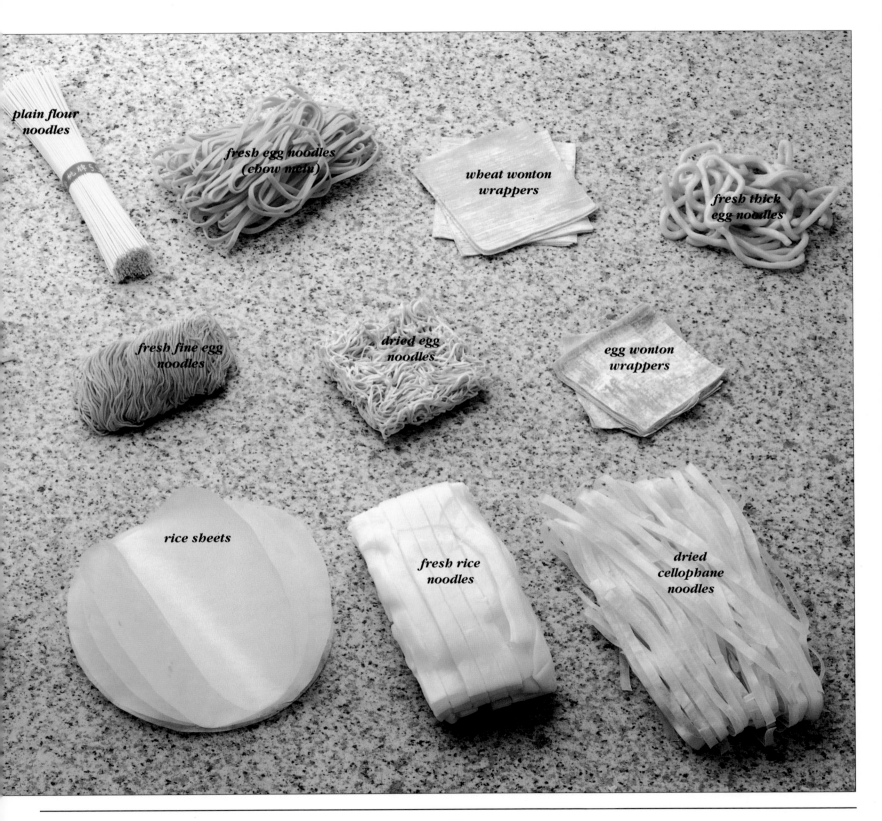

plain flour
noodles

fresh egg noodles
(chow mein)

wheat wonton
wrappers

fresh thick
egg noodles

fresh fine egg
noodles

dried egg
noodles

egg wonton
wrappers

rice sheets

fresh rice
noodles

dried
cellophane
noodles

## Japanese noodles

There are four main types of Japanese noodle, all of which play an important part in its cuisine. Although distinct from Chinese noodles, they share many of the same characteristics, and most Japanese noodles are available from Chinese supermarkets, where they are as popular in Chinese cuisine as they are in Japan.

## Gyoza wrappers

The Japanese equivalent to wonton skins. The wrappers can be filled with ground meat, fish, vegetables and seasonings. They are usually browned on one side, turned and simmered in broth and served as appetizers.

## Harusame noodles

Meaning "spring rain", these transparent noodles are the equivalent to the Chinese cellophane noodles. They can be deep-fried, or soaked and are used in a variety of dishes.

## Soba noodles

Made from a mixture of buckwheat and wheat flour, these noodles are very popular in Japan. Thin and brownish in colour, they are used in soups and are sometimes served cold with garnishes and a dipping sauce. They are best cooked in simmering water for a few minutes, until tender.

## Somen noodles

These are very fine, white noodles made from wheat flour. They come dried, usually tied in bundles, held together with a paper band.

They are ideal in soups, in the popular Japanese one-pot meals and are also often served cold as a summer dish. If they are not available, vermicelli pasta can be used instead.

## Udon noodles

These are the most popular and versatile of Japanese noodles. Like somen noodles, they are made from white wheat flour but are thicker and more substantial. They are normally rounded in shape like spaghetti, although they can be flat.

Udon noodles are available fresh, pre-cooked or dried. Fresh noodles need only a few minutes' cooking in simmering water, for noodles straight from the packet, follow the directions provided. Udon noodles are generally served in hot soups and in mixed meat and vegetable dishes.

## Other noodles: River rice noodles

Made from rice ground with water, these Chinese noodles have been steamed into thin sheets before being cut into ribbons about 1 cm/½ in wide. They can be used in stir-fries or chow mein dishes. If possible, buy fresh noodles, as they have an excellent flavour and texture. Dried noodles should be boiled and drained before use.

## Spring roll wrappers

Thinner and larger than wonton wrappers, these are made from wheat flour and water. There are two types, the Cantonese, which are smooth, like a noodle dough, and the Shanghai, which are transparent, like rice paper.

## Wonton wrappers

These are made from the same dough as egg noodles, namely wheat flour, egg and water, cut into circles and 7.5 cm/3 in squares of varying thicknesses. They are normally sold fresh or frozen; if frozen, they will keep for several months.

---

### NOODLE KNOW-HOW

Dried noodles should be stored in airtight containers, where they can be kept for many months. Fresh noodles will keep in the fridge for 3–4 days, or in an unopened packet until their use-by date. They can also be frozen for up to 6 months.

Quantities will depend not only on appetite but also on whether there are accompanying noodle or rice dishes. If noodles are the principal dish, allow 75–115 g/3–4 oz fresh noodles or one square or oblong of dried noodles per person. The exception is cellophane noodles, which are used more as a vegetable and therefore quantities will generally be smaller. Cellophane noodles may need presoaking for 30 minutes.

*Gyoza wrappers*

*somen noodles*

# Fresh and Store-cupboard Essentials

Almost all ingredients you can think of – and many you wouldn't – can be used in noodle dishes. Many of the traditional oriental ingredients are available in supermarkets or in Asian grocers, so it is possible to make dishes from the East that are absolutely authentic.

## Bamboo shoots

These are available fresh but are more commonly seen canned. They have a fairly bland flavour and are generally used for their crunchy texture. Drain well and rinse under cold water before using in a recipe.

## Beancurd/Tofu

This soya bean product is available in several forms, including soft, firm, silken, grilled, fried and dried. Plain, uncooked beancurd is entirely neutral in taste, absorbing the flavour of other ingredients.

It is low in fat, high in protein and calcium and is therefore a versatile and useful ingredient for healthy, low-calorie meals.

## Beancurd cheese/ Red-fermented beancurd

This deep red beancurd has a very strong and cheesy flavour. It is fermented with salt, red rice and rice wine and is used in Asian cooking for flavouring meat, poultry and vegetarian dishes. It is usually stored in jars or earthenware pots and will keep for several months if refrigerated.

## Beansprouts

Used for their delicious texture in meat and vegetable dishes, cook for only 30 seconds. They will keep for 1–2 days in the fridge, but will discolour and wilt if left any longer.

## Black beans, fermented

These whole soya beans are preserved in salt and ginger. They are pungent in taste but, when cooked in stir-fries or other dishes with additional ingredients, bring a delicious flavour to the meal.

## Bonito

In Japanese cookery, these are the dried flakes of a strongly flavoured tuna. They are used frequently for stocks and soups and can be sprinkled over food as a seasoning.

## Chinese leaves/ Chinese lettuce

The crispy leaves of this vegetable are ideal for stir-frying or for soups. They are particularly popular in the latter, where their crunchy texture contrasts wonderfully with cellophane noodles.

## Chinese mushrooms

These add flavour and texture to numerous Asian dishes. They are almost always sold dried and should be soaked before using. The caps are then sliced or halved, the stems discarded.

## Cloud ears

These Chinese mushrooms are only available dried. After soaking they expand to form thick, brown clusters. They have little or no flavour, absorbing flavours from other seasonings, but are appreciated for their silky but crunchy texture. Rinse well to remove any sand and discard any hard bits.

## Coconut milk/ Coconut cream

Used in almost all Asian cuisine, coconut milk is especially popular in Thai, Indonesian and Malaysian cooking, where it is used extensively, particularly in fish and poultry dishes.

Cans of coconut milk and cream are available from most supermarkets, as well as oriental stores. Buy unsweetened coconut milk. If the recipe calls for sugar, add this yourself.

Creamed coconut is a solid bar of milky-white coconut, which will keep in the fridge for months. Dissolve it in hot or boiling water according to the packet directions.

## Dashi

The name given to the Japanese kombu and bonito stock. Instant dashi is available from Japanese and most large Chinese grocers.

## Enoki mushrooms

These small, cultivated mushrooms have long, thin stems and tiny, white caps. They are harvested in clumps attached at the base, which should be cut off before use. They have a crisp texture and delicate flavour and may be eaten raw or lightly cooked. When using in cooked dishes, add at the last minute, as heating tends to toughen them.

## Fish sauce

This is an essential ingredient in many South East Asian countries, particularly Thailand and Indonesia.

Made from the liquid from salted fermented anchovies, it has a strong aroma and taste. Use sparingly until you acquire the taste.

## Kombu

This popular Japanese ingredient is a type of kelp seaweed and is used to flavour stock. Kombu and bonito flake stock granules are available from Japanese supermarkets, as is a liquid form and a teabag-style instant stock. Kombu can also be served as a vegetable.

## Mooli

Also known as daikon or Chinese radish, this large, white vegetable has a smooth, creamy-white skin and is normally sold with feathery, green tops. It has a pleasant, slightly spicy taste and is excellent steamed, pickled, used in stir-fries and chow mein or thinly sliced and eaten raw.

## Mustard greens/ Mustard cabbage

There are many varieties of mustard greens but the most commonly available and most suitable for cooking, rather than pickling, are those with a pale green stalk and large, single, oval leaf. They have a very distinctive taste and are used in soups and thick stews.

## Nori/Yaki-nori/Ao-nori

Nori is dried seaweed, popular in Japanese and some Thai cooking. It is sold in paper-thin sheets which are dark green to black in colour. It is normally toasted and used as a wrapping for sushi and as a garnish.

Yaki-nori are ready-toasted sheets and ao-nori is a flaked, dried green seaweed used for seasoning. Both are available from oriental stores.

## Oil

The favoured oil in most Asian cooking is groundnut or peanut oil. It has a rich, nutty flavour. However, it is expensive and not widely available and corn oil or sunflower oil can be used as a satisfactory substitute.

Sesame oil, with its distinct, nutty flavour, is made from toasted sesame seeds and is used for stirring into noodles or sprinkling over noodle dishes. It burns easily and is not recommended for cooking; however, a little will add a wonderful, aromatic flavour.

*Right: Just some of the fresh ingredients used in Asian cooking available in large supermarkets.*

## Pak choi

This attractive, cabbage-like vegetable has a long, smooth, milky-white stem and large, dark green leaves.

## Rice vinegar

This is a pale vinegar with a distinct but delicate flavour. It is milder than most other light wine vinegars and is available from oriental stores.

## Rice wine

Chinese rice wine has a rich, sherry-like flavour and is used in marinades or added to stir-fries or fried noodle dishes. It is available from most large super-markets and oriental grocers.

## Sake

This Japanese rice wine is now widely available. It is used occasionally in marinades or at the end of cooking and is frequently served, either hot or chilled, with Japanese meals.

## Shiitake mushrooms

These tasty, firm-textured Japanese mushrooms are available fresh or dried. They have a meaty, slightly acidic flavour and a rather slippery texture. Dried mushrooms should be soaked in hot water for about 20 minutes and then strained. Save the water for the sauce. Add to stir-fries for a delicious flavour and texture.

## Wood ears

These are similar to cloud ears, though larger in size and coarser in texture. Mild in flavour they absorb the taste of the more strongly flavoured ingredients and are used mainly in soups and stir-fries, adding texture and colour.

## Yard-long beans

These are long, thin beans, similar to French beans but three or four times longer. Cut into smaller lengths and use just like ordinary beans.

Available in most oriental stores, choose those that are small and flexible. They can be refrigerated for up to five days.

# Herbs, Spices and Flavourings

Try to keep a selection of these ingredients handy, so that you can rustle up a quick and delicious noodle dish without extensive shopping.

## Chillies

There is a wide range of fresh and dried chillies from which to choose. Generally the larger the chilli, the milder the flavour, although there are exceptions, so be warned!

## Chinese chives

Also known as garlic chives, these have larger leaves than normal chives and have a mild garlic flavour. They need very little cooking, so stir them into a dish just before serving or use raw as a garnish. Look for plump, uniformly green specimens with no brown spots.

## Coriander

Fresh coriander has a distinct flavour, adding an essential pungency to many Chinese or Indonesian-style dishes. Finely or roughly chop and add to a dish, just before serving, or use as a garnish. Bunches of leaves will keep for up to 5 days in a jar of water.

## Cumin

Available as whole seed or ground, cumin has a pungent flavour and is used widely in beef dishes and other dishes requiring a curry flavour. Store in a cool, dark place for no more than six months.

## Dried shrimps

Not to be confused with our own prawns, these are small, shelled shrimps that have been salted and dried in the sun. They have a strong, fishy taste and are used as a seasoning for meat and vegetables in Chinese, Thai and Indonesian cooking. Rinse under cold water before use.

## Dried shrimp paste or Shrimp sauce

Made from ground shrimps fermented in brine, this has a strong aroma and flavour and is used in Chinese, Thai and Malaysian cuisine to enhance seafood dishes. It is usually sold in jars and will keep almost indefinitely in a cool place.

## Five-spice powder

A pungent mixture of cloves, cinnamon, fennel, star anise and Szechuan pepper, used extensively in Chinese cooking.

## Galangal

This rhizome is reminiscent of ginger, pine and citrus and is similar in appearance to ginger, except that it is thinner and the young shoots are bright pink.

Peel in the same way as fresh root ginger and add to sauces and curries. Remove from the dish before serving.

## Ginger

This is another essential ingredient in Asian cookery, used for its warm, fresh flavour and pleasant spiciness. Fresh root ginger is widely available and cannot be substituted with ground ginger. Choose ginger with a firm, unblemished skin, peel with a sharp knife and then finely chop or grate according to the recipe.

## Kaffir lime leaves

Also known simply as lime leaves, these add a unique flavour and are excellent in marinades, as well as stir-fries and sauces. The leaves need to be bruised to release the flavour, by rubbing between your fingers. If fresh leaves are not available, dried leaves can be used instead.

## Lemon grass

This aromatic herb has a thin, tapering stem and a citrusy, verbena flavour. To use, thinly slice the bulb end of the root and add to marinades or sauces according to the recipe.

## Mirin

Sweet cooking sake, this has a delicate flavour and is usually added in the final stages of cooking.

## Seven-flavour spice or Shichimi

Used in Japanese cooking, this has a noticeably oriental tang. It is made of sansho, seaweed, chilli, tangerine peel, poppy seeds and white and black sesame seeds.

## Soy sauce

Made from fermented soya beans, together with salt, sugar and yeast, this is one of the most ancient and popular seasonings in oriental cookery. There are three main types: Chinese dark or thick soy sauce and light or thin soy sauce, and Japanese soy sauce.

Dark soy sauce, which gives a reddish-brown hue to food, is used for meatier 'red-braised' dishes. Light soy sauce is thinner in consistency and paler in colour. It still has a salty flavour, but is used for paler dishes, such as chicken or fish. Japanese soy sauce (also called shoyu) is lighter in flavour than Chinese soy sauces and is best used when making the more delicate Japanese food.

## Star anise

This spice has a pungent, aniseed flavour and is used either ground or whole.

## Szechuan chilli paste/ Chilli paste

This hot paste of dried red chillies and ground yellow bean sauce is wonderful in fish dishes.

## Tamarind

The brown, sticky pulp of the bean-like seed pod of the tamarind tree. The pulp is usually diluted with water and strained before use. Tamarind has a sour, yet fruity taste, resembling sour prunes.

*Right: Experiment with the wonderful array of Asian herbs and spices available today.*

# Equipment

You will find most of the cooking equipment you have around the kitchen will be all you need. A wok is probably the most useful item, although even that is not essential, as a large frying pan can be substituted. However, if you are interested in investing in authentic tools of the trade, consider some of the following:

### Bamboo skewers
These are widely used for barbecues and grilled foods. They should be soaked before use, and then discarded afterwards.

### Chopping board
A good-quality chopping board with a thick surface is essential and will last for years.

### Citrus zester
This tool is designed to remove the rind or zest of citrus fruit, while leaving the bitter white pith. It can also be used for shaving fresh coconut.

### Cleaver
The weight of the cleaver makes it ideal for chopping all kinds of ingredients. Keep this as sharp as possible.

### Cooking chopsticks
These are extra-long and allow you to stir ingredients in the wok while keeping a safe distance.

### Draining wire
This is designed to sit on the side of the wok and is used mainly when deep-frying.

### Food processor
Useful for numerous kitchen tasks, this is a quick alternative to the pestle and mortar.

### Knives
It is very important to use the right-sized knife for the job, for safety and for efficiency. There are two essential knives that should be in every kitchen. A chopping knife with a heavy, wide blade about 18–20 cm/7–8 in long is ideal for chopping vegetables, meats and fresh herbs. A paring knife has a smaller blade and is necessary for trimming and peeling vegetables and fruits.

### Ladle
A long-handled ladle is very useful for spooning out soups, stock and sauces.

### Pestle and mortar
A deep granite pestle and mortar is ideal for crushing garlic, ginger and herbs to a paste or for grinding small amounts of spices.

### Rice paddle
Used to fluff up rice after cooking.

### Saucepan
A good saucepan with a tight-fitting lid is essential for cooking rice properly.

### Sharpening stone
A traditional tool for sharpening knives and cleavers. It is available from hardware stores.

### Stainless-steel skimmer
This can be used when strong flavours are likely to affect bare-metal cooking implements.

### Wire skimmer
This is the Asian alternative to a slotted spoon and one or the other is absolutely essential in Asian cooking. Use for removing cooked food from boiling water or hot fat. However, it should not be used with fish-based liquids as the strong flavour is likely to react with the metal.

### Wok
The shape of the wok allows ingredients to be cooked in a minimum of fat, thus retaining freshness and flavour. There are several varieties available, including the carbon-steel, round-bottomed or Pau wok. A round-bottomed wok is best suited to a gas hob, where you will be able to control the amount of heat needed more easily. The carbon-steel, flat-bottomed wok is best for electric or solid-fuel hobs as it gives a better heat distribution.

Warm the wok gently before adding the oil for cooking. The oil then floods easily over the warm pan and prevents food from sticking.

*wok*

*cooking chopsticks*

*stainless-steel skimmers*

*la*

food processor

bamboo skewers

saucepan

chopping
board

draining
wire

chopping
knife

sharpening
stone

citrus
zester

cleavers

pestle and
mortar

rice paddle

wire skimmer

# Basic Techniques

## Preparing Lemon Grass

Use the whole stem and remove it before cooking or chop the root.

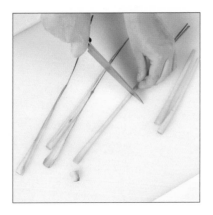

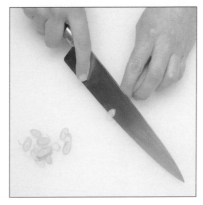

**1** Cut off and discard the dry, leafy tops. Peel away any tough outer layers. Trim off the tops and end of the stem until you are left with about 10 cm/4 in.

**2** Lay the lemon grass on a board. Set the flat side of a chef's knife on top and strike it firmly with your fist. Cut across the lemon grass to make thin slices.

## Preparing Kaffir Lime Leaves

The distinctive lime-lemon aroma and flavour of Kaffir lime leaves are a vital part of Thai cooking.

### COOK'S TIP
Buy fresh lime leaves in oriental stores and freeze them for future use. Dried lime leaves are also now available.

**1** You can tear, shred or cut kaffir lime leaves. Using a small, sharp knife, carefully remove the centre vein. Cut the leaves crossways into very fine strips.

## Preparing Fresh Ginger

Fresh root ginger can be used in slices, strips or finely chopped.

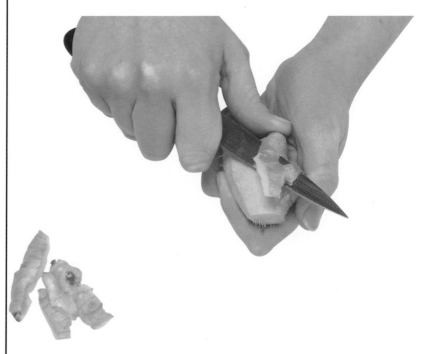

**1** Using a small, sharp knife, peel the skin from the root ginger.

**2** Place the ginger on a board, set the flat side of a cleaver or chef's knife on top and strike it firmly with your fist – this will soften the fibrous texture.

**3** Chop the ginger as coarsely or finely as you wish, moving the blade backwards and forwards.

# Preparing Beansprouts

Usually available from supermarkets, beansprouts add a crisp texture to stir-fries.

**1** Pick over the beansprouts, discarding any pieces that are discoloured, broken or wilted.

**2** Rinse the beansprouts under cold running water and drain well.

# Preparing Spring Onions

Use spring onions in stir-fries to flavour oil, as a vegetable in their own right, or as a garnish.

**1** Trim off the root and any discoloured tops with a sharp knife. For an intense flavour in a stir-fry, cut the entire spring onion into thin matchsticks.

**2** Alternatively, slice the white and pale green part of the spring onion diagonally and stir-fry with crushed garlic, to flavour the cooking oil.

# Chopping Coriander

Chop coriander just before you use it, the flavour will then be much better.

**1** Strip the leaves from the stalks and pile them on a chopping board.

**2** Using a cleaver or chef's knife, cut the coriander into small pieces, moving the blade back and forth until it is as coarsely or finely chopped as you wish.

# Preparing Chillies

The flavour of chilli is wonderful in cooking, but fresh chillies must be handled with care.

**1** Wearing rubber gloves, remove the stalks from the chillies.

**2** Cut in half lengthways. Scrape out the seeds and fleshy, white pith from each half, using a sharp knife. Chop or thinly slice according to the recipe.

# Seasoning a Wok

If you are using a new wok or frying pan, you will need to prepare it as follows, to ensure the best results described below.

**1** A brand new wok will probably have been given a protective coating of oil by the manufacturer, which will need to be removed before seasoning. To do this, scrub the wok with a cream cleanser, rinse thoroughly and dry.

To season the wok, place it over a low heat and add 30 ml/2 tbsp vegetable oil. Using a pad of kitchen paper, rub the entire inside of the wok with the oil, then heat slowly for 10–15 minutes.

**2** Using a pad of kitchen paper, rub the entire inside of the wok with the oil, then heat slowly for 10–15 minutes.

**3** Alternatively add 30–45 ml/2–3 tbsp salt to the wok and heat slowly for the same length of time.

**4** Wipe the inside of the wok clean with more kitchen paper; the paper will become black. Repeat the process of coating, heating and wiping several times until the paper is no longer blackened. The wok is now seasoned and will have a good non-stick surface; do not scrub it again.

## COOK'S TIP

To keep a seasoned wok clean, just wash it in hot water without detergent, then wipe it dry. The wok may rust if not in constant use. If it does, scour the rust off and repeat the seasoning process.

# Deep-frying

The advantage of a wok is that it can be used for deep-frying as well as stir-frying. It uses far less oil than a deep fat fryer.

**1** Put the wok on a stand and half fill with oil. Heat until the required temperature registers on a thermometer. Alternatively, test by dropping in a small piece of food: if bubbles form all over the surface, the oil is ready.

**2** Carefully add the food to the oil using long wooden chopsticks or tongs, and move it around to prevent it sticking together. Using a bamboo strainer or slotted spoon, carefully remove the food and drain on kitchen paper before serving. Make sure that the wok is fully secure on its stand before adding the oil. Never leave the wok unattended.

# Stir-frying

Many noodle recipes, such as chow mein, involve stir-frying. A wok is the perfect piece of equipment for this type of cooking.

**1** Prepare all the ingredients before you start cooking, using a small, sharp knife to cut the vegetables into even-sized pieces. Meat should be cut into thin slices against the grain. It may be easier to slice meat if it has been frozen slightly for an hour or so beforehand. By the time you have sliced it, the meat will be ready to cook.

**2** Cutting all the ingredients to a uniform size often means that the preparation of ingredients for stir-frying may take longer than the cooking itself. Once ready, it is important to make sure that all the ingredients are close to hand as wok cooking needs constant attention. Heat the wok for a few minutes before adding the oil.

**3** When the pan is hot, add the oil and swirl it or brush it around to coat the base and sides of the wok. Allow the oil to heat for a few moments.

**4** Reduce the heat a little, as you add the first ingredients, to ensure they do not burn and that aromatics, like garlic and spring onions, do not become bitter. Stir-fry over quite a high heat, but not so high that food sticks and burns.

**5** Foods should be added in a specific order, usually aromatics first (garlic, ginger, spring onions), followed by the main ingredients which require some cooking, such as meats and denser vegetables and then the finer ingredients. Keep the ingredients moving in the pan with a long-handled spatula or wooden spoon. If the ingredients in the wok begin to dry out, add a splash of water.

## COOK'S TIP
The advantage of cooking with a wok is that its gently sloping sides allow the heat to spread rapidly and evenly over the surface, enabling food to cook quickly, retaining flavour, colour and nutrients.

# Pork Satay with Crispy Noodle Cake

Crispy noodles are a popular and tasty accompaniment to satay, and are particularly good with the spicy satay sauce.

*Serves 4–6*

INGREDIENTS
450 g/1 lb lean pork
3 garlic cloves, finely chopped
15 ml/1 tbsp Thai curry powder
5 ml/1 tsp ground cumin
5 ml/1 tsp sugar
15 ml/1 tbsp fish sauce
90 ml/6 tbsp oil
350 g/12 oz thin egg noodles
fresh coriander, to garnish

FOR THE SATAY SAUCE
30 ml/2 tbsp oil
2 garlic cloves, finely chopped
1 small onion, finely chopped
2.5 ml/½ tsp hot chilli powder
5 ml/1 tsp Thai curry powder
250 ml/8 fl oz/1 cup coconut milk
15 ml/1 tbsp fish sauce
30 ml/2 tbsp sugar
juice of ½ lemon
165 g/5½ oz crunchy peanut butter

*pork*

*garlic*

*Thai curry powder*

*onion*

*ground cumin*

*sugar*

*fish sauce*

*egg noodles*

*fresh coriander*

*hot chilli powder*

*coconut milk*

*lemon*

*crunchy peanut butter*

**1** Cut the pork into thin 5-cm/2-in-long strips. Mix the garlic, curry powder, cumin, sugar and fish sauce in a bowl. Stir in about 30 ml/2 tbsp of the oil. Add the meat to the bowl, toss to coat and leave to marinate in a cool place for at least 2 hours. Meanwhile cook the noodles in a large saucepan of boiling water until just tender. Drain thoroughly.

**2** Make the satay sauce. Heat the oil in a saucepan and fry the garlic and onion with the chilli powder and curry powder for 2–3 minutes. Stir in the coconut milk, fish sauce, sugar, lemon juice and peanut butter. Mix well. Reduce the heat and cook, stirring frequently, for about 20 minutes or until the sauce thickens. Be careful not to let the sauce stick to the bottom of the pan or it will burn.

**3** Heat about 15 ml/1 tbsp of the remaining oil in a frying pan. Spread the noodles evenly over the pan and fry for 4–5 minutes until crisp and golden. Turn the noodle cake over carefully and cook the other side until crisp. Keep hot.

**4** Drain the meat and thread it on to the drained skewers. Cook under a hot grill for 8–10 minutes until cooked, turning occasionally and brushing with the remaining oil. Serve with wedges of noodle cake, accompanied by the satay sauce. Garnish with coriander leaves.

# Vegetable Spring Rolls with Sweet Chilli Sauce

Vermicelli noodles need hardly any cooking before stirring into the tasty vegetable filling.

*Makes 20–24*

INGREDIENTS
25 g/1 oz rice vermicelli noodles
oil, for deep-frying
5 ml/1 tsp grated fresh root ginger
2 spring onions, finely shredded
50 g/2 oz carrot, finely grated
50 g/2 oz mangetouts, thinly sliced
25 g/1 oz young spinach leaves
50 g/2 oz/¼ cup beansprouts
15 ml/1 tbsp chopped fresh mint
15 ml/1 tbsp chopped fresh
    coriander
30 ml/2 tbsp fish sauce
20–24 spring roll wrappers,
    each 13 cm/5 in square
1 egg white, lightly beaten

FOR THE DIPPING SAUCE
50 g/2 oz/4 tbsp caster sugar
50 ml/3½ tbsp rice vinegar
2 red chillies, seeded and finely
    chopped

*rice vermicelli noodles*

*spring onions*

*mangetouts*

*fresh coriander*

*beansprouts*

*fish sauce*

*spring roll wrappers*

*red chillies*

COOK'S TIP
Use groundnut oil for this recipe or otherwise sunflower oil. Groundnut oil has a distinct flavour and gives an authentic taste. Sunflower oil is milder but still very good.

**1** First make the dipping sauce: place the sugar and vinegar in a small pan with 30 ml/2 tbsp water. Heat gently, stirring until the sugar dissolves, then boil rapidly until it forms a light syrup. Stir in the chillies and leave to cool.

**2** Soak the noodles according to the packet instructions; rinse and drain well. Using scissors, snip the noodles into short lengths.

**3** Heat 15 ml/1 tbsp of the oil in a wok and stir-fry the ginger and spring onions for 15 seconds. Add the carrot and mangetouts and stir-fry for 2–3 minutes. Add the spinach, beansprouts, mint, coriander, fish sauce and noodles and stir-fry for a further minute. Set aside.

**4** Take one spring roll wrapper and arrange it so that it faces you in a diamond shape. Place a spoonful of filling just below the centre, then fold up the bottom point over the filling.

**5** Fold in each side, then roll up tightly. Brush the end with beaten egg white to seal. Repeat this process until all the filling has been used.

**6** Half-fill a wok with oil and heat to 180°C/350°F. Deep-fry the spring rolls in batches for 3–4 minutes until golden. Drain. Serve hot with the chilli sauce.

# Japanese Chilled Noodles with Dashi Dip

This classic Japanese dish of cold noodles is known as *somen*. The noodles are surprisingly refreshing when eaten with fish or fried meats and the delicately flavoured dip.

## Serves 4–6

INGREDIENTS
15–30 ml/1–2 tbsp oil
2 medium eggs, beaten with a pinch
 of salt
1 sheet yaki-nori seaweed, finely
 shredded
½ bunch spring onions, thinly sliced
wasabi paste
400 g/14 oz dried somen noodles
ice cubes, for serving

FOR THE DIP
1 litre/1¾ pints/4 cups kombu and
 bonito stock or instant dashi
200 ml/7 fl oz/scant 1 cup Japanese
 soy sauce
15 ml/1 tbsp mirin

*eggs*

*spring onions*

*wasabi paste*

*mirin*

*kombu and bonito stock*

*soy sauce*

*dried somen noodles*

**1** Prepare the dashi dip in advance so that it has time to cool and chill. Using either kombu and bonito stock or instant dashi, bring all the ingredients to the boil. Leave to cool and chill thoroughly.

Meanwhile, heat a little oil in a frying pan. Pour in half the beaten eggs, tilting the pan to coat the base evenly. Leave to set, then turn the omelette over and cook the second side briefly. Turn out on to a board. Cook the remaining egg in the same way.

**2** Leave the omelettes to cool and then shred them finely. Place the shredded omelette, yaki nori, spring onions and wasabi in four small bowls.

**3** Boil the somen noodles according to the packet instructions and drain. Rinse the noodles thoroughly under cold, running water, stirring with chopsticks, then drain thoroughly again.

**4** Place the noodles on a large plate and add some ice cubes on top to keep them cool. Pour the cold dip into four small bowls. Noodles and accompaniments are dipped into the chilled dip before they are eaten.

# Chinese-style Cabbage and Noodle Parcels

The noodles and Chinese mushrooms give a delightful oriental flavour to these traditional cabbage rolls. Serve with rice for a tasty meal.

*Serves 4–6*

### INGREDIENTS
4 dried Chinese mushrooms, soaked
 in hot water until soft
50 g/2 oz cellophane noodles,
 soaked in hot water until soft
450 g/1 lb minced pork
2 garlic cloves, finely chopped
8 spring onions
30 ml/2 tbsp fish sauce
12 large outer green cabbage leaves

### FOR THE SAUCE
30 ml/2 tbsp oil
1 small onion, finely chopped
2 garlic cloves, crushed
400 g/14 oz can chopped plum
 tomatoes
pinch of sugar
salt and freshly ground black pepper

*Chinese mushrooms*

*spring onions*

*cellophane noodles*

*minced pork*

*garlic*   *fish sauce*   *onion*

*chopped plum tomatoes*

**1** Drain the mushrooms, discard the stems and chop the caps. Put them in a bowl. Next, drain the noodles and cut them into short lengths. Add to the bowl with the pork and garlic. Chop two of the spring onions and add to the bowl. Season with the fish sauce and pepper.

**2** Blanch the cabbage leaves a few at a time in a saucepan of boiling, salted water for about 1 minute. Remove the leaves from the pan and refresh under cold water. Drain and dry on kitchen paper. Blanch the remaining six spring onions in the same fashion. Drain well. Fill one of the cabbage leaves with a generous spoonful of the pork and noodle filling. Taking hold of the corner closest to yourself, roll up the leaf sufficiently to enclose the filling, then tuck in the sides and continue rolling the leaf to make a tight parcel. Make more parcels in the same way.

**3** Split each spring onion lengthways by cutting through the bulb and then tearing upwards. Tie each of the cabbage parcels with a length of spring onion.

**4** To make the sauce, heat the oil in a large frying pan and add the onion and garlic. Fry for 2 minutes until soft. Tip the plum tomatoes into a bowl. Mash with a fork then add to the onion mixture.

**5** Season the tomato mixture with salt, pepper and a pinch of sugar, then bring to simmering point. Add the cabbage parcels. Cover and cook gently for 20–25 minutes or until the filling is cooked. Taste the sauce to check the seasoning and serve at once.

### COOK'S TIP
If at any time the tomato sauce looks a little dry, add some water or vegetable stock to the pan and stir through.

# Thai Pork Spring Rolls

Crunchy spring rolls are as popular in Thai cuisine as they are in Chinese. In this version they are filled with noodles, garlic and pork.

## *Makes about 24*

INGREDIENTS

4–6 dried Chinese mushrooms,
    soaked in hot water until soft
50 g/2 oz cellophane noodles
30 ml/2 tbsp oil
2 garlic cloves, chopped
2 red chillies, seeded and chopped
225 g/8 oz minced pork
50 g/2 oz cooked peeled prawns,
    chopped
30 ml/2 tbsp fish sauce
5 ml/1 tsp sugar
freshly ground black pepper
1 carrot, very finely sliced
50 g/2 oz bamboo shoots, chopped
50 g/2 oz/¼ cup beansprouts
2 spring onions, chopped
15 ml/1 tbsp chopped fresh coriander
30 ml/2 tbsp plain flour
24 x 15 cm/6 in square spring roll
    wrappers
oil, for deep-frying
Thai sweet chilli sauce, to serve
    (optional)

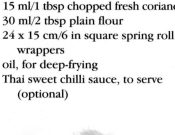
*Chinese mushrooms* *cellophane noodles* *garlic*

*minced pork* *cooked prawns* *fish sauce*

*beansprouts* *fresh coriander* *spring roll wrappers*

**1** Drain and finely chop the Chinese mushrooms. Remove and discard the stems. Soak the noodles in hot water until soft, then drain. Cut into short lengths, about 5 cm/2 in.

**2** Heat the oil in a wok or large frying pan, add the garlic and chillies and fry for 30 seconds. Add the pork and stir-fry for a few minutes until the meat is browned. Add the noodles, mushrooms and prawns. Season with fish sauce, sugar and pepper. Tip into a bowl. Add the carrot, bamboo shoots, beansprouts, spring onions and coriander and stir well to mix.

**3** Put the flour in a small bowl and blend with a little water to make a paste. Place a spoonful of filling in the centre of a spring roll wrapper.

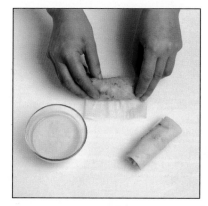

**4** Turn the bottom edge over to cover the filling, then fold in the left and right sides. Roll the wrapper up almost to the top edge. Brush the top edge with flour paste and seal. Repeat with the rest of the wrappers.

**5** Heat the oil in a wok or deep-fat fryer. Slide in the spring rolls a few at a time and fry until crisp and golden brown. Remove with a slotted spoon and drain on kitchen paper. Serve with Thai sweet chilli sauce to dip them into, if liked.

# Fried Monkfish Coated with Rice Noodles

These marinated medallions of fish are coated in rice vermicelli and deep-fried – they taste as good as they look.

*Serves 4*

INGREDIENTS
450 g/1 lb monkfish
5 ml/1 tsp grated fresh root ginger
1 garlic clove, finely chopped
30 ml/2 tbsp light soy sauce
175 g/6 oz rice vermicelli noodles
50 g/2 oz cornflour
2 eggs, beaten
oil, for deep-frying
banana leaves, to serve (optional)

FOR THE DIPPING SAUCE
30 ml/2 tbsp light soy sauce
30 ml/2 tbsp rice vinegar
15 ml/1 tbsp sugar
salt and freshly ground black pepper
2 red chillies, seeded and thinly
    sliced
1 spring onion, thinly sliced

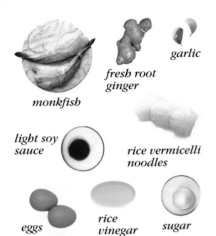

*monkfish*

*fresh root ginger*

*garlic*

*light soy sauce*

*rice vermicelli noodles*

*eggs*

*rice vinegar*

*sugar*

*red chillies*

*spring onion*

**1** Cut the monkfish into 2.5-cm/1-in-thick medallions. Place in a dish and add the ginger, garlic and soy sauce. Leave to marinate for 10 minutes. For the dipping sauce, heat the soy sauce, vinegar and sugar in a saucepan until boiling. Add the salt and pepper. Remove from the heat, add the chillies and spring onion.

**2** Using kitchen scissors, cut the noodles into 4-cm/1½-in lengths. Spread them out in a shallow bowl.

**3** Coat the fish medallions in cornflour, dip in beaten egg and cover with noodles, pressing them on to the fish so that they stick.

**4** Deep-fry the coated fish in hot oil, 2–3 pieces at a time, until the noodle coating is crisp and golden brown. Drain and serve hot on banana leaves if you like, accompanied by the dipping sauce.

# Deep-fried Wonton Cushions with Sambal Kecap

These delicious, golden packages, called *pansit goreng*, are popular in Indonesia as party fare or for a quick snack.

*Makes 40*

INGREDIENTS
115 g/4 oz pork fillet, trimmed and sliced
225 g/8 oz cooked peeled prawns
2–3 garlic cloves, crushed
2 spring onions, roughly chopped
15 ml/1 tbsp cornflour
about 40 wonton wrappers
oil, for deep-frying
salt and freshly ground black pepper

FOR THE SAMBAL KECAP
1–2 red chillies, seeded and sliced
1–2 garlic cloves, crushed
45 ml/3 tbsp dark soy sauce
45–60 ml/3–4 tbsp lemon or lime juice

*cornflour*

*pork fillet*

*cooked prawns*

*garlic*

*spring onions*

*wonton wrappers*

*red chillies*

*lemon juice*

*dark soy sauce*

**1** Grind the slices of pork finely in a food processor. Add the prawns, garlic, spring onions and cornflour. Season to taste and then process briefly.

**2** Place a little of the prepared filling on to each wonton wrapper, just off centre, with the wrapper positioned like a diamond in front of you. Dampen all the edges, except for the uppermost corner of the diamond.

**3** Lift the corner nearest to you towards the filling and then roll up the wrapper, to cover the filling. Turn over. Bring the two extreme corners together, sealing one on top of the other. Squeeze lightly, to plump up the filling. Repeat the process until all the wrappers and the filling are used up. The prepared 'cushions' and any leftover wonton wrappers can be frozen at this stage.

**4** Meanwhile, prepare the sambal. Mix the chillies and garlic together and then stir in the dark soy sauce, lemon or lime juice and 15–30 ml/1–2 tbsp water. Pour into a serving bowl and set aside.

**5** Deep-fry the wonton cushions in hot oil, a few at a time, for about 2–3 minutes, or until cooked through, crisp and golden brown. Serve on a large platter together with the sambal kecap.

# Alfalfa Crab Salad with Crispy Fried Noodles

The crispy noodles make a delicious contrast, both in flavour and texture, with this healthy mixture of crab and vegetables.

*Serves 4–6*

### INGREDIENTS

oil, for deep-frying
50 g/2 oz Chinese rice noodles
150 g/5 oz frozen white crab meat, thawed
115 g/4 oz/½ cup alfalfa sprouts
1 small iceberg lettuce
4 sprigs fresh coriander, roughly chopped
1 ripe tomato, skinned, seeded and diced
4 sprigs fresh mint, roughly chopped, plus an extra sprig to garnish

### FOR THE SESAME LIME DRESSING

45 ml/3 tbsp vegetable oil
5 ml/1 tsp sesame oil
½ small red chilli, seeded and finely chopped
1 piece stem ginger in syrup, cut into matchsticks
10 ml/2 tsp stem ginger syrup
10 ml/2 tsp light soy sauce
juice of ½ lime

*Chinese rice noodles*
*crab meat*
*alfalfa sprouts*
*iceberg lettuce*
*tomato*
*mint*
*fresh coriander*
*red chilli*
*lime juice*

**1** First make the dressing: combine the vegetable and sesame oils in a bowl. Add the chilli, stem ginger, stem ginger syrup and soy sauce and stir in the lime juice. Set aside.

**2** Heat the oil in a wok or deep-fat fryer to 196°C/385°F. Fry the noodles, one handful at a time, until crisp. Lift out and drain on kitchen paper.

**3** Flake the white crab meat into a bowl and toss with the alfalfa sprouts.

**4** Finely chop the lettuce and mix with the coriander, tomato and mint. Place in a bowl, top with the noodles and the crab meat and alfalfa salad and garnish with a sprig of mint. Serve with the sesame lime dressing.

# Smoked Trout and Noodle Salad

This salad is a wonderful example of how well noodles can combine with Mediterranean ingredients, such as trout, capers and tomato.

*Serves 4*

INGREDIENTS
225 g/8 oz somen noodles
2 smoked trout, skinned and boned
2 hard-boiled eggs, coarsely
    chopped
30 ml/2 tbsp snipped chives
lime halves, to serve (optional)

FOR THE DRESSING
6 ripe plum tomatoes
2 shallots, finely chopped
30 ml/2 tbsp tiny capers, rinsed
30 ml/2 tbsp chopped fresh
    tarragon
finely grated rind and juice of
    ½ orange
60 ml/4 tbsp extra-virgin olive oil
salt and freshly ground black pepper

*somen noodles*  *smoked trout*  *chives*

*hard-boiled eggs*  *olive oil*  *orange juice and grated rind*

*plum tomatoes*  *shallots*

*fresh tarragon*

**1** To make the dressing, cut the tomatoes in half, remove the cores and cut the flesh into chunks. Place in a bowl with the shallots, capers, tarragon, orange rind, orange juice and olive oil. Season with salt and pepper, and mix well. Leave the dressing to marinate for 1–2 hours.

**2** Cook the noodles in a large saucepan of boiling water until just tender. Drain and rinse under cold, running water. Drain well.

## COOK'S TIP
Choose tomatoes that are firm, bright in colour and have a matt texture, avoiding any with blotched or cracked skins.

**3** Toss the noodles with the dressing, then adjust the seasoning to taste. Arrange the noodles on a large serving platter or individual plates.

**4** Flake the smoked trout over the noodles, then sprinkle the coarsely chopped eggs and snipped chives over the top. Serve the lime halves on the side, if you like.

# Beef Noodle Soup

This rich, satisfying soup is packed with all sorts of flavours and textures, brought together with delicious egg noodles.

## Serves 4

INGREDIENTS

10 g/¼ oz dried porcini mushrooms
6 spring onions
115 g/4 oz carrots
350 g/12 oz rump steak
about 30 ml/2 tbsp oil
1 garlic clove, crushed
2.5 cm/1 in fresh root ginger,
    finely chopped
1.2 litres/2 pints/5 cups beef stock
45 ml/3 tbsp light soy sauce
60 ml/4 tbsp dry sherry
75 g/3 oz thin egg noodles
75 g/3 oz spinach, shredded
salt and freshly ground black pepper

dried porcini mushrooms

spring onions

carrots

rump steak

garlic

fresh root ginger

beef stock

dry sherry

egg noodles

light soy sauce

spinach

**1** Break the mushrooms into small pieces, place in a bowl and pour over 150 ml/¼ pint/⅔ cup boiling water. Leave to soak for 15 minutes.

**2** Cut the spring onions and carrots into 5-cm/2-in-long, fine strips. Trim any fat off the meat and slice into thin strips.

**3** Heat the oil in a large saucepan and cook the beef in batches until browned, adding a little more oil if necessary. Remove the beef with a slotted spoon and drain on kitchen paper.

**4** Add the garlic, ginger, spring onions and carrots to the pan and stir-fry for 3 minutes.

**5** Add the beef stock, the mushrooms and their soaking liquid, the soy sauce, sherry and plenty of seasoning. Bring to the boil and simmer, covered, for 10 minutes.

**6** Break up the noodles slightly and add to the pan, with the spinach. Simmer gently for 5 minutes, or until the beef is tender. Adjust the seasoning before serving.

# Chiang Mai Noodle Soup

A signature dish of the Thai city of Chiang Mai, this richly flavoured and aromatic noodle soup has Burmese origins.

## *Serves 4–6*

INGREDIENTS
600 ml/1 pint/2½ cups coconut milk
30 ml/2 tbsp red curry paste
5 ml/1 tsp ground turmeric
450 g/1 lb chicken thighs, boned
    and cut into bite-size chunks
600 ml/1 pint/2½ cups chicken stock
60 ml/4 tbsp fish sauce
15 ml/1 tbsp dark soy sauce
juice of ½–1 lime
450 g/1 lb fresh egg noodles,
    blanched briefly in boiling water
salt and freshly ground black pepper

FOR THE GARNISH
3 spring onions, chopped
4 red chillies
4 shallots, chopped
60 ml/4 tbsp sliced pickled mustard
    leaves, rinsed
30 ml/2 tbsp fried sliced garlic
fresh coriander sprigs

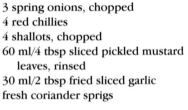
*coconut milk*   *red curry paste*   *ground turmeric*

*chicken thighs*   *chicken stock*

*fish sauce*   *dark soy sauce*   *lime*   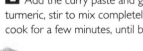 *fresh egg noodles*

 *red chillies*    *spring onions*    *fresh coriander*

**1** Pour about one third of the coconut milk into a saucepan and bring to the boil, stirring frequently until it separates.

**2** Add the curry paste and ground turmeric, stir to mix completely and cook for a few minutes, until blended.

**3** Add the chicken pieces to the saucepan and stir-fry for about 2 minutes. Ensure that all the chunks of meat are coated with the paste.

**4** Add the remaining coconut milk, stock, fish sauce, soy sauce and seasoning. Simmer for 7–10 minutes. Remove from the heat and add the lime juice.

Reheat the noodles in boiling water, then drain. Divide the noodles and chicken among the bowls and ladle over the hot soup. Top with the garnishes.

# Pork and Pickled Mustard Greens Soup

The pickled mustard leaves give the flavour while the cellophane noodles bring texture to this traditional Thai soup.

*Serves 4–6*

INGREDIENTS

225 g/8 oz pickled mustard leaves, soaked
50 g/2 oz cellophane noodles, soaked
15 ml/1 tbsp oil
4 garlic cloves, finely sliced
1 litre/1¾ pints/4 cups chicken stock
450 g/1 lb pork ribs, cut into large chunks
30 ml/2 tbsp fish sauce
pinch of sugar
freshly ground black pepper
2 red chillies, seeded and finely sliced, to garnish

*cellophane noodles*

*garlic*

*chicken stock*

*pork ribs*

*fish sauce*

*red chillies*

**1** Drain the pickled mustard leaves and cut them into bite-size pieces. Taste to check the seasoning is to your liking. If they are too salty, soak them in water for a little bit longer.

**2** Drain the cellophane noodles and cut them into short lengths.

**3** Heat the oil in a small frying pan, add the garlic and stir-fry until golden, taking care not to let it burn. Transfer the mixture to a bowl and set aside.

**4** Put the stock in a saucepan, bring to the boil, then add the pork and simmer gently for 10–15 minutes. Add the pickled mustard leaves and cellophane noodles. Bring back to the boil. Season to taste with fish sauce, sugar and freshly ground black pepper. Serve hot, topped with the fried garlic and red chillies.

# Hanoi Beef and Noodle Soup

Millions of North Vietnamese eat this fragrant noodle soup every day for breakfast.

## Serves 4–6

INGREDIENTS
1 onion
1.5 kg/3–3½ lb stewing beef
2.5 cm/1 in fresh root ginger, peeled
1 star anise
1 bay leaf
2 whole cloves
2.5 ml/½ tsp fennel seeds
1 piece cassia or cinnamon stick
fish sauce, to taste
juice of 1 lime
150 g/5 oz fillet steak
450 g/1 lb fresh flat rice noodles
salt and freshly ground black pepper
handful of fresh coriander leaves
    and lime wedges, to garnish

FOR THE ACCOMPANIMENTS
1 small red onion, sliced into rings
115 g/4 oz/½ cup beansprouts
2 red chillies, seeded and sliced
2 spring onions, finely sliced

**1** Cut the onion in half. Grill under a high heat, cut side up, until the exposed sides are caramelized and deep brown.

**2** Cut the stewing beef into large chunks and then place in a large saucepan or stock pot. Add the caramelized onion with the ginger, star anise, bay leaf, cloves, fennel seeds and cassia or cinnamon stick.

**3** Add 3 litres/5 pints/12½ cups water, bring to the boil, reduce the heat and simmer gently for 2–3 hours, skimming off the fat and scum from time to time.

stewing beef

fresh root ginger

star anise

bay leaf

whole cloves

fennel seeds

cassia

fish sauce

lime

fillet steak

fresh rice noodles

fresh coriander

onion

beansprouts

red chillies

spring onions

**4** Using a slotted spoon, remove the meat from the stock; when cool enough to handle, cut into small pieces. Strain the stock and return to the pan or stock pot together with the meat. Bring back to the boil and season with the fish sauce, lime juice and salt and pepper to taste.

**5** Slice the fillet steak very thinly and then chill until required. Cook the noodles in a large pan of boiling water until just tender. Drain and divide among individual serving bowls. Arrange the thinly sliced steak over the noodles, pour the hot stock on top and garnish with coriander and lime wedges. Serve, offering the accompaniments in separate bowls.

# Malaysian Spicy Prawn and Noodle Soup

This is a Malaysian version of Hanoi Beef and Noodle Soup using fish and prawns instead of beef. If laksa noodles aren't available, flat rice noodles can be used instead.

*Serves 4–6*

### INGREDIENTS

25 g/1 oz unsalted cashew nuts
3 shallots, or 1 medium onion, sliced
5 cm/2 in lemon grass, shredded
2 cloves garlic, crushed
30 ml/2 tbsp oil
1 cm/½ in cube shrimp paste or 15 ml/1 tbsp fish sauce
15 ml/1 tbsp mild curry paste
400 ml/14 fl oz/1⅔ cups coconut milk
½ chicken stock cube
3 curry leaves (optional)
450 g/1 lb white fish fillets, e.g. cod, haddock or whiting
225 g/8 oz prawns, fresh or cooked
150 g/5 oz laksa noodles, soaked for 10 minutes before cooking
1 small cos lettuce, shredded
115 g/4 oz/½ cup beansprouts
3 spring onions, cut into lengths
½ cucumber, thinly sliced
prawn crackers, to serve

*cashew nuts (unsalted)*
*garlic*
*shrimp paste*
*curry paste*
*coconut milk*
*curry leaves*
*white fish fillets*
*prawns*
*laksa noodles*
*lemon grass*
*beansprouts*
*spring onions*
*cucumber*
*shallots*

## COOK'S TIP

To serve, line a serving platter with the lettuce leaves. Arrange all the ingredients, including the beansprouts, spring onions, cucumber and prawn crackers, in neat piles. Serve the soup from a large tureen or stoneware pot.

**1** Grind the cashew nuts using a pestle and mortar and then spoon into a food processor and process with the shallots or onion, lemon grass and garlic.

**2** Heat the oil in a large wok or saucepan, add the cashew and onion mixture, and fry for about 1–2 minutes, until the mixture begins to brown.

**3** Add the shrimp paste or fish sauce and curry paste, followed by the coconut milk, stock cube and curry leaves, if using. Simmer for 10 minutes.

**4** Cut the white fish into bite-size pieces. Add the fish and prawns in the coconut stock, immersing them with a frying basket or a slotted spoon. Cook for 3–4 minutes until the fish is tender. Cook the noodles according to the instructions on the packet.

# Cheat's Shark's Fin Soup

Shark's fin soup is a renowned delicacy. In this vegetarian version cellophane noodles mimic shark's fin needles.

## Serves 4–6

### Ingredients

4 dried Chinese mushrooms
25 ml/1½ tbsp dried wood ears
115 g/4 oz cellophane noodles
30 ml/2 tbsp oil
2 carrots, cut into fine strips
115 g/4 oz canned bamboo shoots, rinsed, drained and cut into fine strips
1 litre/1¾ pints/4 cups vegetable stock
15 ml/1 tbsp light soy sauce
15 ml/1 tbsp arrowroot or potato flour
1 egg white, beaten (optional)
5 ml/1 tsp sesame oil
salt and freshly ground black pepper
2 spring onions, finely chopped, to garnish
Chinese red vinegar, to serve (optional)

*dried Chinese mushrooms*

*dried wood ears*

*cellophane noodles*

*carrots*

*bamboo shoots*

*vegetable stock*

*light soy sauce*

*egg*

*sesame oil*

*spring onions*

**1** Soak the mushrooms and wood ears separately in warm water for 20 minutes. Drain. Remove the mushroom stems and slice the caps thinly. Cut the wood ears into fine strips, discarding any hard bits. Soak the noodles in hot water until soft. Drain and cut into short lengths.

**2** Heat the oil in a large saucepan. Add the mushrooms and stir-fry for 2 minutes. Add the wood ears, stir-fry for 2 minutes, then stir in the carrots, bamboo shoots and noodles.

**3** Add the stock to the pan. Bring to the boil, then simmer for 15–20 minutes.

**4** Season with salt, pepper and soy sauce. Blend the arrowroot or potato flour with about 30 ml/2 tbsp water. Pour into the soup, stirring all the time to prevent lumps from forming as the soup continues to simmer.

**5** Remove the pan from the heat. Stir in the egg white, if using, so that it sets to form small threads in the hot soup. Stir in the sesame oil, then pour the soup into individual bowls. Sprinkle each portion with chopped spring onions and offer the Chinese red vinegar separately, if using.

# Noodles, Chicken and Prawns in Coconut Broth

This dish takes a well-flavoured broth and adds noodles and a delicious combination of other ingredients to make a satisfying main course.

*Serves 8*

INGREDIENTS
2 onions, quartered
2.5 cm/1 in fresh root ginger, sliced
2 garlic cloves
4 macadamia nuts or 8 almonds
1–2 chillies, seeded and sliced
2 lemon grass stems, lower
    5 cm/2 in sliced
5 cm/2 in fresh turmeric, peeled and
    sliced, or 5 ml/1 tsp ground
    turmeric
15 ml/1 tbsp coriander seeds,
    dry-fried
5 ml/1 tsp cumin seeds, dry-fried
60 ml/4 tbsp oil
400 ml/14 fl oz/1⅔ cups coconut
    milk
1.5 litres/2½ pints/6¼ cups chicken
    stock
375 g/13 oz rice noodles, soaked in
    cold water
350 g/12 oz cooked tiger prawns
salt and freshly ground black pepper

FOR THE GARNISH
4 hard-boiled eggs, quartered
225 g/8 oz cooked chicken, chopped
225 g/8 oz/1 cup beansprouts
1 bunch spring onions, shredded
deep-fried onions (optional)

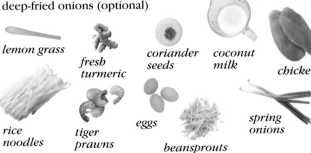

*lemon grass*

*fresh turmeric*

*coriander seeds*

*coconut milk*

*chicken*

*rice noodles*

*tiger prawns*

*eggs*

*beansprouts*

*spring onions*

**1** Place the quartered onions, ginger, garlic and nuts in a food processor with the chillies, sliced lemon grass and turmeric. Process to a paste. Alternatively, pound all the ingredients with a pestle and mortar. Grind the coriander and cumin seeds coarsely and add to the paste.

**2** Heat the oil in a pan and fry the spice paste, without colouring, to bring out the flavours. Add the coconut milk, stock and seasoning and simmer for 5–10 minutes.

**3** Meanwhile, drain the rice noodles and plunge them into a large pan of salted, boiling water for 2 minutes. Remove from the heat and drain well. Rinse thoroughly with plenty of cold water, to halt the cooking process.

**4** Add the tiger prawns to the soup just before serving and heat through for a minute or two. Arrange the garnishes in separate bowls. Each person helps themselves to noodles, adds soup, eggs, chicken and beansprouts and then scatters shredded spring onions and deep-fried onions, if liked, on top.

## COOK'S TIP

To dry-fry spices, heat a small heavy-based pan over a medium heat for 1 minute, add the spices and cook for 2–3 minutes, stirring frequently. Remove from the heat and grind the spices using a mortar and pestle.

# Beef Soup with Noodles and Meatballs

Egg noodles and spicy meatballs make this a really sustaining main meal soup. In the east it is often served from street stalls.

*Serves 6*

## INGREDIENTS

450 g/1 lb dried medium egg noodles
45 ml/3 tbsp sunflower oil
1 large onion, finely sliced
2 garlic cloves, crushed
2.5 cm/1 in fresh root ginger, cut into thin matchsticks
1.2 litres/2 pints/5 cups beef stock
30 ml/2 tbsp dark soy sauce
2 celery sticks, finely sliced, leaves reserved
6 Chinese leaves, cut into bite-size pieces
1 handful mangetouts, cut into strips
salt and freshly ground black pepper

## FOR THE MEATBALLS

1 large onion, roughly chopped
1–2 red chillies, seeded and chopped
2 garlic cloves, crushed
1 cm/½ in cube shrimp paste
450 g/1 lb lean minced beef
15 ml/1 tbsp ground coriander
5 ml/1 tsp ground cumin
10 ml/2 tsp dark soy sauce
5 ml/1 tsp dark brown sugar
juice of ½ lemon
a little beaten egg

**dark soy sauce**

**egg**

red chillies

garlic

ground coriander

ground cumin

**dark brown sugar**

**lemon juice**

**minced beef**

**onion**

**mangetouts**

**fresh root ginger**

**Chinese leaves**

**celery**

**dried egg noodles**

**beef stock**

### COOK'S TIP
Shrimp paste, or *terasi*, has a strong, salty, distinctive flavour and smell. Use sparingly if unsure of its flavour.

**1** For the meatballs, put the onion, chillies, garlic and shrimp paste in a food processor. Process in short bursts, taking care not to over-chop the onion.

**2** Put the meat in a large bowl. Stir in the onion mixture. Add the ground coriander and cumin, soy sauce, sugar, lemon juice and seasoning.

**3** Bind the mixture with a little beaten egg and shape into small balls.

**4** Cook the noodles in a large pan of boiling, salted water for 3–4 minutes, or until *al dente*. Drain in a colander and rinse with plenty of cold water. Set aside. Heat the oil in a wide pan and fry the onion, garlic and ginger until soft but not browned. Add the stock and soy sauce and bring to the boil.

**5** Add the meatballs, half-cover and simmer until they are cooked, about 5–8 minutes. Just before serving, add the sliced celery and, after 2 minutes, the Chinese leaves and mangetouts. Adjust the seasoning. Divide the noodles among soup bowls, pour the soup on top and garnish with the reserved celery leaves.

# Japanese Noodle Casseroles

Traditionally these individual casseroles are cooked in earthenware pots. *Nabe* means "pot" and *yaki* means "to heat", providing the Japanese title of *nabeyaki udon* for this recipe.

## Serves 4

INGREDIENTS
115 g/4 oz boneless chicken thighs
2.5 ml/½ tsp salt
2.5 ml/½ tsp sake or dry white wine
2.5 ml/½ tsp light soy sauce
1 leek
115 g/4 oz fresh spinach, trimmed
300 g/11 oz dried udon noodles or
    500 g/1¼ lb fresh udon noodles
4 shiitake mushrooms, stems
    removed
4 medium eggs
shichimi or seven-flavour spice, to
    serve (optional)

FOR THE SOUP
1.4 litres/2⅓ pints/6 cups kombu and
    bonito stock or instant dashi
25 ml/1½ tbsp light soy sauce
5 ml/1 tsp salt
15 ml/1 tbsp mirin

light soy sauce · leek · chicken thighs · sake · spinach · shiitake mushrooms · udon noodles · eggs · kombu and bonito stock · mirin

**1** Cut the chicken into small chunks and sprinkle with the salt, sake or wine and soy sauce. Cut the leek diagonally into 4-cm/1½-in slices.

**2** Boil the spinach for 1–2 minutes, then drain and soak in cold water for 1 minute. Drain, squeeze lightly, then cut into 4-cm/1½-in lengths. If using dried udon noodles, boil them according to the packet instructions, allowing 3 minutes less than the stated cooking time. Place fresh udon noodles in boiling water, disentangle, then drain.

**5** Divide the spinach among the casseroles and simmer, covered, for a further 1 minute.

**6** Serve immediately, standing the hot casseroles on plates or table mats. Sprinkle seven-flavour spice over the casseroles if liked.

**3** For the soup, bring the kombu and bonito stock, soy sauce, salt and mirin to the boil in a saucepan and add the chicken and leek. Skim the broth, then simmer for 5 minutes.

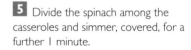

**4** Divide the udon noodles among four individual flameproof casseroles. Pour the soup, chicken and leeks into the casseroles. Place over a moderate heat and add the shiitake mushrooms. Gently break an egg into each casserole. Cover and simmer gently for 2 minutes.

## COOK'S TIP

Assorted tempura using vegetables, such as sweet potato, carrot and shiitake mushrooms, and fish such as squid and prawns could be served in these casseroles instead of chicken and egg.

# Crispy Noodles with Mixed Vegetables

In this dish, rice vermicelli noodles are deep-fried until crisp, then tossed into a colourful selection of stir-fried vegetables.

*Serves 3–4*

### INGREDIENTS

2 large carrots
2 courgettes
4 spring onions
115 g/4 oz yard-long beans or green beans
115 g/4 oz dried rice vermicelli or cellophane noodles
oil, for deep-frying
2.5 cm/1 in fresh root ginger, cut into shreds
1 red chilli, seeded and sliced
115 g/4 oz fresh shiitake or button mushrooms, thickly sliced
a few Chinese cabbage leaves, coarsely shredded
75 g/3 oz/⅓ cup beansprouts
30 ml/2 tbsp light soy sauce
30 ml/2 tbsp Chinese rice wine
5 ml/1 tsp sugar
30 ml/2 tbsp roughly torn coriander leaves

*carrots*

*spring onions*

*yard-long beans*

*dried rice vermicelli noodles*

*fresh root ginger*

*red chillies*

*shiitake mushrooms*

*Chinese cabbage*

*beansprouts*

*light soy sauce*

*courgettes*

*Chinese rice wine*

*fresh coriander*

## COOK'S TIP
If a milder flavour is preferred, remove the seeds from the chilli.

**1** Cut the carrots and courgettes into fine sticks. Shred the spring onions into similar-size pieces. Trim the beans. If using yard-long beans, cut them into short lengths.

**2** Break the noodles into lengths of about 7.5 cm/3 in. Half-fill a wok with oil and heat it to 180°C/350°F. Deep-fry the raw noodles, a handful at a time, for 1–2 minutes, until puffed and crispy. Drain on kitchen paper. Carefully pour off all but 30 ml/2 tbsp of the oil.

**3** Reheat the oil in the wok. When hot, add the beans and stir-fry for 2–3 minutes. Add the ginger, red chilli, mushrooms, carrots and courgettes and stir-fry for 1–2 minutes.

**4** Add the Chinese cabbage, beansprouts and spring onions. Stir-fry for 1 minute, then add the soy sauce, rice wine and sugar. Cook, stirring, for about 30 seconds.

**5** Add the noodles and coriander and toss to mix, taking care not to crush the noodles too much. Serve at once, piled up on a plate.

# Chinese Mushrooms with Cellophane Noodles

Red fermented beancurd adds extra flavour to this hearty vegetarian dish. It is brick red in colour, with a very strong, cheesy flavour.

*Serves 3–4*

INGREDIENTS
115 g/4 oz dried Chinese
    mushrooms
25 g/1 oz dried wood ears
115 g/4 oz dried beancurd
30 ml/2 tbsp oil
2 garlic cloves, finely chopped
2 slices fresh root ginger, finely
    chopped
10 Szechuan peppercorns, crushed
15 ml/1 tbsp red fermented
    beancurd
½ star anise
pinch of sugar
15-30 ml/1–2 tbsp dark soy sauce
50 g/2 oz cellophane noodles,
    soaked in hot water until soft
salt

**dried Chinese mushrooms**

**dried wood ears**

**fresh root ginger**

**Szechuan peppercorns**

**star anise**

**dark soy sauce**

**cellophane noodles**

**1** Soak the Chinese mushrooms and wood ears separately in bowls of hot water for 30 minutes. Break the dried beancurd into pieces and soak in water according to the packet instructions.

**2** Strain the mushrooms, squeezing as much liquid from them as possible. Reserve the liquid. Discard the stems and cut the caps in half if they are large. Drain the wood ears, rinse and drain again. Cut off any gritty parts, then cut each wood ear into two or three pieces.

**3** Heat the oil in a heavy-based pan and fry the garlic, ginger and Szechuan peppercorns for a few seconds. Add the mushrooms and red fermented beancurd, mix lightly and fry for 5 minutes.

**4** Add the reserved mushroom liquid to the pan, with sufficient water to completely cover the mushrooms. Add the star anise, sugar and soy sauce, then cover and simmer for 30 seconds. Add the chopped wood ears and reconstituted beancurd pieces to the pan. Cover and cook for about 10 minutes.

**5** Drain the cellophane noodles, add them to the mixture and cook for a further 10 minutes until tender, adding more liquid if necessary. Add salt to taste and serve.

# Stir-fried Beancurd with Noodles

This is a satisfying dish, which is both tasty and easy to make.

*Serves 4*

INGREDIENTS

225 g/8 oz firm beancurd
groundnut oil, for deep-frying
175 g/6 oz medium egg noodles
15 ml/1 tbsp sesame oil
5 ml/1 tsp cornflour
10 ml/2 tsp dark soy sauce
30 ml/2 tbsp Chinese rice wine
5 ml/1 tsp sugar
6–8 spring onions, cut diagonally
    into 2.5-cm/1-in lengths
3 garlic cloves, sliced
1 green chilli, seeded and sliced
115 g/4 oz Chinese cabbage leaves,
    coarsely shredded
50 g/2 oz/¼ cup beansprouts
50 g/2 oz/½ cup cashew nuts,
    toasted

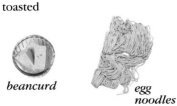

*beancurd*

*egg noodles*

*sesame oil*

*dark soy sauce*

*garlic*

*spring onions*

*Chinese cabbage*

*green chilli*

*beansprouts*

*cashew nuts*

**1** If in water, drain the beancurd and pat dry with kitchen paper. Cut it into 2.5-cm/1-in cubes. Half-fill a wok with groundnut oil and heat to 180°C/350°F. Deep-fry the beancurd in batches for 1–2 minutes, until golden and crisp. Drain on kitchen paper. Carefully pour all but 30 ml/2 tbsp of the oil from the wok.

**2** Cook the noodles. Rinse them thoroughly under cold water and drain well. Toss in 10 ml/2 tsp of the sesame oil and set aside. In a bowl, blend together the cornflour, soy sauce, rice wine, sugar and remaining sesame oil.

**3** Reheat the 30 ml/2 tbsp of groundnut oil and, when hot, add the spring onions, garlic, chilli, Chinese cabbage and beansprouts. Stir-fry for 1–2 minutes.

**4** Add the beancurd, noodles and cornflour sauce. Cook, stirring, for about 1 minute, until well mixed. Sprinkle over the cashew nuts. Serve at once.

# Egg Noodle Stir-fry

The thick egg noodles and potatoes, along with the vegetables, make this a satisfying and healthy main dish. If possible, use fresh egg noodles, which are available from most large supermarkets.

*Serves 4*

INGREDIENTS

2 eggs
5 ml/1 tsp chilli powder
5 ml/1 tsp ground turmeric
60 ml/4 tbsp oil
1 large onion, finely sliced
2 red chillies, seeded and finely sliced
15 ml/1 tbsp light soy sauce
2 large cooked potatoes, cut into small cubes
6 pieces fried beancurd, sliced
225 g/8 oz/1 cup beansprouts
115 g/4 oz green beans, blanched
350 g/12 oz fresh thick egg noodles
salt and freshly ground black pepper
sliced spring onions, to garnish

 *eggs*

*chilli powder*

*ground turmeric*

 *onion*

*red chillies*

*light soy sauce*

*potatoes*

*fried beancurd*

 *bean sprouts*

 *green beans*

*fresh thick egg noodles*

 *spring onions*

## COOK'S TIP

Ideally wear gloves when preparing chillies; if you don't, certainly wash your hands thoroughly afterwards. Keep your hands away from your eyes as chillies will sting them.

**1** Beat the eggs lightly, then strain them into a bowl. Heat a lightly greased omelette pan. Pour in half of the beaten egg to just thinly cover the bottom of the pan. When the egg is set, carefully turn the omelette over and fry the other side briefly.

**2** Slide the omelette on to a plate, blot with kitchen paper, roll up and cut into narrow strips. Make a second omelette in the same way and slice. Set the omelette strips aside for the garnish.

**3** In a cup, mix together the chilli powder and turmeric. Form a paste by stirring in a little water. Heat the oil in a wok or large frying pan. Fry the onion until soft. Reduce the heat and add the chilli paste, sliced chillies and soy sauce. Fry for 2–3 minutes.

**4** Add the potatoes and fry for about 2 minutes, mixing well with the chillies. Add the beancurd, then the beansprouts, green beans and noodles.

**5** Gently stir-fry until the noodles are evenly coated and heated through. Take care not to break up the potatoes or the beancurd. Season with salt and pepper. Serve hot, garnished with the reserved omelette strips and spring onion slices.

# Peanut and Vegetable Noodles

Add any of your favourite vegetables to this recipe, which is quick to make for a great mid-week supper.

*Serves 3–4*

INGREDIENTS
225 g/8 oz medium egg noodles
30 ml/2 tbsp olive oil
2 garlic cloves, crushed
1 large onion, roughly chopped
1 red pepper, seeded and roughly
    chopped
1 yellow pepper, seeded and
    roughly chopped
350 g/12 oz courgettes, roughly
    chopped
150 g/5 oz/generous ½ cup roasted
    unsalted peanuts, roughly
    chopped

FOR THE DRESSING
60 ml/4 tbsp olive oil
grated rind and juice of 1 lemon
1 red chilli, seeded and finely
    chopped
45 ml/3 tbsp chopped fresh chives,
    plus extra to garnish
15–30 ml/1–2 tbsp balsamic vinegar
salt and white pepper

*egg noodles*   *garlic*   *onion*
*red pepper*   *yellow pepper*
*courgettes*   *peanuts*   *red chilli*
*chives*   *lemon*

**1** Soak the noodles according to the packet instructions and drain well.

**2** Meanwhile, heat the oil in a very large frying pan or wok and cook the garlic and onion for 3–4 minutes, until beginning to soften. Add the peppers and courgettes and cook for a further 15 minutes over a medium heat, until beginning to soften and brown. Add the peanuts and cook for a further 1 minute.

**3** Make the dressing. In a bowl, whisk together the olive oil, grated lemon rind and 45 ml/3 tbsp lemon juice, the chilli, the chopped fresh chives, plenty of salt and pepper to season and balsamic vinegar to taste.

**4** Toss the noodles into the vegetables and stir-fry to heat through. Add the dressing, stir to coat thoroughly and serve immediately, garnished with chopped fresh chives.

# Five-spice Vegetable Noodles

Vary this vegetable stir-fry by substituting mushrooms, bamboo shoots, beansprouts, mangetouts or water chestnuts for some or all of the vegetables suggested below.

*Serves 3–4*

INGREDIENTS

225 g/8 oz dried thin or medium
   egg noodles
30 ml/2 tbsp sesame oil
2 carrots
1 celery stick
1 small fennel bulb
2 courgettes, halved and sliced
1 red chilli, seeded and chopped
2.5 cm/1 in fresh root ginger, grated
1 garlic clove, crushed
7.5 ml/1½ tsp Chinese five-spice
   powder
2.5 ml/½ tsp ground cinnamon
4 spring onions, sliced
sliced red chilli, to garnish (optional)

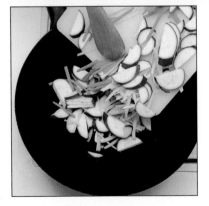

*celery stick*

*egg noodles*

*carrots*

*fennel bulb*

*courgettes*

*red chilli*

*fresh root ginger*

*five-spice powder*

*garlic*

*cinnamon*

*spring onions*

**1** Bring a large pan of salted water to the boil. Add the noodles and cook for 2–3 minutes until just tender. Drain the noodles, return them to the pan and toss in a little of the oil. Set aside.

**2** Cut the carrot and celery into julienne strips. Cut the fennel bulb in half and cut away the hard core. Cut into slices, then cut the slices into thin strips.

**3** Heat the remaining oil in a wok until very hot. Add all the vegetables, including the chopped chilli, and stir-fry for 7–8 minutes. Add the ginger and garlic and stir-fry for 2 minutes, then add the spices. Cook for 1 minute.

**4** Add the spring onions, stir-fry for 1 minute and then stir in 60 ml/4 tbsp warm water and cook for 1 minute. Stir in the noodles and toss well together. Serve sprinkled with sliced red chilli, if liked.

# Noodles with Asparagus and Saffron Sauce

The asparagus, wine and cream give a distinctly French flavour to this elegant and delicious noodle dish.

*Serves 4*

INGREDIENTS
450 g/1 lb young asparagus
25 g/1 oz/2 tbsp butter
2 shallots, finely chopped
30 ml/2 tbsp white wine
250 ml/8 fl oz/1 cup double cream
pinch of saffron threads
grated rind and juice of ½ lemon
115 g/4 oz/1 cup garden peas
350 g/12 oz somen noodles
½ bunch chervil, roughly chopped
salt and freshly ground black pepper
grated Parmesan cheese (optional)

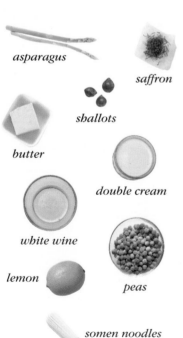

*asparagus*

*saffron*

*shallots*

*butter*

*double cream*

*white wine*

*lemon*

*peas*

*somen noodles*

**1** Cut off the asparagus tips (about 5 cm/2 in length), then slice the remaining spears into short rounds. Soak the saffron in 30 ml/2 tbsp boiling water for a few minutes until softened.

Melt the butter in a saucepan, add the shallots and cook over a low heat for 3 minutes, until soft. Add the white wine, cream and saffron infusion. Bring to the boil, reduce the heat and simmer gently for 5 minutes or until the sauce thickens to a coating consistency. Add the lemon rind and juice, with salt and pepper to taste.

**2** Bring a large saucepan of lightly salted water to the boil. Blanch the asparagus tips, scoop them out and add them to the sauce, then cook the peas and short asparagus rounds in the boiling water until just tender. Scoop them out and add to the sauce.

**3** Cook the somen noodles in the same water until just tender, following the directions on the packet. Drain, place in a wide pan and pour the sauce over the top.

**4** Toss the noodles with the sauce and vegetables, adding the chervil and more salt and pepper if needed. Finally, sprinkle with the grated Parmesan, if using, and serve hot.

## COOK'S TIP
Frozen peas can easily be used instead of fresh peas. Add to the asparagus after 3–4 minutes and cook until tender.

# Fried Noodles with Beansprouts and Baby Asparagus

This dish is simplicity itself with a wonderful contrast of textures and flavours. Use young asparagus which is beautifully tender and cooks in minutes.

*Serves 2*

INGREDIENTS
115 g/4 oz dried thin or medium
    egg noodles
60 ml/4 tbsp oil
1 small onion, chopped
2.5 cm/1 in fresh root ginger, grated
2 garlic cloves, crushed
175 g/6 oz young asparagus,
    trimmed
115 g/4 oz/½ cup beansprouts
4 spring onions, sliced
45 ml/3 tbsp light soy sauce
salt and freshly ground black pepper

*egg noodles*     *onion*

*garlic*

*fresh root
ginger*

*beansprouts*

*asparagus*     *spring
onions*     *light soy
sauce*

**1** Bring a pan of salted water to the boil. Add the noodles and cook for 2–3 minutes, until just tender. Drain and toss in 30 ml/2 tbsp of the oil.

**2** Heat the remaining oil in a wok or frying pan until very hot. Add the onion, ginger and garlic and stir-fry for 2–3 minutes. Add the asparagus and stir-fry for a further 2–3 minutes.

**3** Add the noodles and beansprouts and stir-fry for 2 minutes.

**4** Stir in the spring onions and soy sauce. Season to taste, adding salt sparingly as the soy sauce will add quite a salty flavour. Stir-fry for 1 minute, then serve at once.

# Vegetable Chow Mein with Cashew Nuts

Chow mein is a popular dish that can be served with almost any type of Chinese vegetarian, meat or fish dish.

### Serves 3–4

INGREDIENTS
30 ml/2 tbsp oil
50 g/2 oz/½ cup cashew nuts
2 carrots, cut into thin strips
3 celery sticks, cut into thin strips
1 green pepper, seeded and cut into
    thin strips
225 g/8 oz/1 cup beansprouts
225 g/8 oz dried medium or thin
    egg noodles
30 ml/2 tbsp toasted sesame seeds,
    to garnish

FOR THE LEMON SAUCE
30 ml/2 tbsp light soy sauce
15 ml/1 tbsp dry sherry
150 ml/¼ pint/⅔ cup vegetable stock
2 lemons
15 ml/1 tbsp sugar
10 ml/2 tsp cornflour

**cashew nuts**

**carrots**

**green pepper**

**beansprouts**

**dried egg noodles**

**toasted sesame seeds**

**light soy sauce**

**lemon**

**1** Stir all the ingredients for the lemon sauce together in a jug. Bring a large saucepan of salted water to the boil.

**2** Heat the oil in a wok or large heavy-based frying pan. Add the cashew nuts, toss quickly over a high heat until golden, then remove with a slotted spoon.

**3** Add the carrots and celery to the pan and stir-fry for 4–5 minutes. Add the pepper and beansprouts and stir-fry for 2–3 minutes more. At the same time, cook the noodles in the pan of boiling water for 3 minutes, or according to the instructions on the packet. Drain well and place in a warmed serving dish.

**4** Remove the vegetables from the pan with a slotted spoon. Pour in the sauce and cook for 2 minutes, stirring until thick. Return the vegetables to the pan, add the cashew nuts and stir quickly to coat in the sauce.

**5** Spoon the vegetables and sauce over the noodles. Scatter with sesame seeds and serve.

# Rice Noodles with Beef and Black Bean Sauce

This is an excellent combination – tender beef with a chilli black bean sauce tossed with silky-smooth rice noodles.

*Serves 4*

INGREDIENTS

450 g/1 lb fresh rice noodles
60 ml/4 tbsp oil
1 onion, finely sliced
2 garlic cloves, finely chopped
2 slices fresh root ginger, finely
    chopped
225 g/8 oz mixed peppers, seeded
    and sliced
350 g/12 oz rump steak, finely sliced
    against the grain
45 ml/3 tbsp fermented black beans,
    rinsed in warm water, drained
    and chopped
30 ml/2 tbsp dark soy sauce
30 ml/2 tbsp oyster sauce
15 ml/1 tbsp chilli black bean sauce
15 ml/1 tbsp cornflour
120 ml/4 fl oz/½ cup beef stock
    or water
2 spring onions, finely chopped,
    and 2 red chillies, seeded and
    finely sliced, to garnish

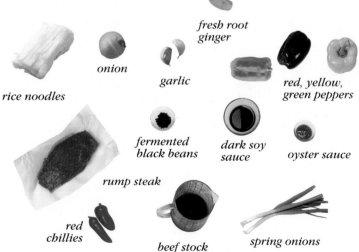

rice noodles

onion

garlic

*fresh root
ginger*

*red, yellow,
green peppers*

*fermented
black beans*

*dark soy
sauce*

*oyster sauce*

*rump steak*

*red
chillies*

*beef stock*

*spring onions*

**1** Rinse the noodles under hot water and drain well. Heat half the oil in a wok or frying pan, swirling it around. Add the onion, garlic, ginger and pepper slices.

**2** Stir-fry for 3–5 minutes until the noodles are heated through, then remove and keep warm. Add the remaining oil to the wok and swirl to coat the pan. When hot, add the sliced beef and fermented black beans and stir-fry over a high heat for 5 minutes or until they are cooked.

**3** In a small bowl, blend the soy sauce, oyster sauce and chilli black bean sauce with the cornflour and stock or water and stir until smooth. Add the mixture to the wok, together with the onion and peppers and cook, stirring, for 1 minute.

**4** Add the noodles and mix lightly. Stir over a medium heat until the noodles are heated through. Adjust the seasoning if necessary. Serve at once, garnished with the chopped spring onions and finely sliced chillies.

# Pork Chow Mein

*Chow mein* is a Cantonese speciality in which noodles are fried either by themselves or, as here, with meat and vegetables.

### Serves 2–3

INGREDIENTS

175 g/6 oz medium egg noodles
350 g/12 oz pork fillet
30 ml/2 tbsp sunflower oil
15 ml/1 tbsp sesame oil
2 garlic cloves, crushed
8 spring onions, sliced
1 red pepper, seeded and roughly
    chopped
1 green pepper, seeded and roughly
    chopped
30 ml/2 tbsp dark soy sauce
45 ml/3 tbsp dry sherry
175 g/6 oz/¾ cup beansprouts
45 ml/3 tbsp chopped fresh flat-leaf
    parsley
15 ml/1 tbsp toasted sesame seeds

*egg noodles*

*pork fillet*

*garlic*

*spring onions*

*sesame oil*

*red pepper*

*green pepper*

*dark soy sauce*

*dry sherry*

*beansprouts*

*flat-leaf parsley*

*toasted sesame seeds*

**1** Soak the noodles according to the packet instructions. Drain well.

**2** Thinly slice the pork fillet. Heat the sunflower oil in a wok or large frying pan and cook the pork over a high heat until golden brown and cooked through.

**3** Add the sesame oil to the pan, with the garlic, spring onions and peppers. Cook over a high heat for 3–4 minutes, or until the vegetables begin to soften.

**4** Reduce the heat slightly and stir in the noodles, with the soy sauce and sherry. Stir-fry for 2 minutes. Add the beansprouts and cook for a further 1–2 minutes. Stir in the parsley and serve sprinkled with the sesame seeds.

# Singapore Noodles

A delicious supper dish with a stunning mix of flavours and textures.

## Serves 3–4

### INGREDIENTS

225 g/8 oz dried egg noodles
45 ml/3 tbsp groundnut oil
1 onion, chopped
2.5 cm/1 in fresh root ginger, finely chopped
1 garlic clove, finely chopped
15 ml/1 tbsp Madras curry powder
2.5 ml/½ tsp salt
115 g/4 oz cooked chicken or pork, finely shredded
115 g/4 oz cooked peeled prawns
115 g/4 oz Chinese cabbage leaves, shredded
115 g/4 oz/½ cup beansprouts
60 ml/4 tbsp chicken stock
15–30 ml/1–2 tbsp dark soy sauce
1–2 red chillies, seeded and finely shredded
4 spring onions, thinly sliced

*dried egg noodles* · *onion* · *fresh root ginger*

*garlic* · *curry powder* · *chicken*

*prawns* · *Chinese cabbage* · *beansprouts*

 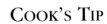 

*chicken stock* · *dark soy sauce* · *red chillies*

*spring onions*

**1** Cook the noodles according to the packet instructions. Rinse thoroughly under cold water and drain well. Toss in 15 ml/1 tbsp of the oil and set aside.

**2** Heat a wok until hot, add the remaining oil and swirl it around. Add the onion, ginger and garlic and stir-fry for about 2 minutes.

## COOK'S TIP

If possible use groundnut oil for this dish or, alternatively, toss the noodles in sesame oil.

**3** Add the curry powder and salt, stir-fry for 30 seconds, then add the egg noodles, chicken or pork and prawns. Stir-fry for 3–4 minutes.

**4** Add the Chinese cabbage and beansprouts and stir-fry for 1–2 minutes. Stir in the stock and soy sauce to taste and toss well until evenly mixed. Serve at once, sprinkled with the shredded red chillies and spring onions.

# Thai Fried Noodles

A staple of day-to-day Thai life, this dish is often served from the many food stalls that line any Thai street.

## *Serves 4*

INGREDIENTS

175 g/6 oz ribbon rice noodles
30 ml/2 tbsp oil
2 garlic cloves, crushed
115 g/4 oz pork fillet, finely
    chopped
2 canned anchovy fillets, chopped
30 ml/2 tbsp lemon juice
45 ml/3 tbsp fish sauce
15 ml/1 tbsp caster sugar
225 g/8 oz beancurd, cubed
2 eggs, beaten
75 g/3 oz cooked peeled prawns
115 g/4 oz/½ cup beansprouts
75 g/3 oz/½ cup unsalted roasted
    peanuts
75 ml/5 tbsp chopped fresh
    coriander
fresh coriander sprigs, to garnish
    (optional)
dried flaked chillies and fish sauce,
    to serve

*ribbon rice noodles*    *garlic*    *pork fillet*
*anchovy fillets*    *lemon juice*    *fish sauce*
*caster sugar*    *beancurd*    *eggs*
*prawns*    *beansprouts*    *peanuts*    *fresh coriander*    *dried flaked chillies*

**1** Soak the noodles in boiling water, according to the packet instructions; drain well.

**2** Heat the oil in a wok or large frying pan and cook the garlic until golden. Add the pork and stir-fry until cooked through and golden.

**3** Reduce the heat slightly and stir in the anchovies, lemon juice, fish sauce and sugar. Bring to a gentle simmer.

**4** Stir in the beancurd, taking care not to break it up. Fold in the noodles gently, until they are coated in the liquid.

**5** Make a gap at the side of the pan and add the beaten eggs. Allow them to scramble slightly and then stir them into the noodles.

**6** Stir in the prawns and most of the beansprouts, peanuts and coriander. Cook until piping hot. Serve the noodles topped with the remaining beansprouts, peanuts and chopped coriander, sprinkled with a few dried flaked chillies and more fish sauce, to taste. Garnish with fresh coriander sprigs, if liked.

# Five-flavour Noodles

The Japanese title for this dish is *gomoku yakisoba*, meaning five different ingredients: noodles, pork, cabbage, beansprouts and peppers.

## *Serves 4*

INGREDIENTS

300 g/11 oz dried Chinese thin egg
   noodles or 500 g/1¼ lb fresh
   yakisoba noodles
200 g/7 oz pork fillet, thinly sliced
25 ml/1½ tbsp oil
10 g/¼ oz fresh root ginger, grated
1 garlic clove, crushed
200 g/7 oz/1¾ cups green cabbage,
   roughly chopped
115 g/4 oz/½ cup beansprouts
1 green pepper, seeded and cut into
   fine strips
1 red pepper, seeded and cut into
   fine strips
salt and freshly ground black pepper
20 ml/4 tsp ao-nori seaweed, to
   garnish (optional)

FOR THE SEASONING

60 ml/4 tbsp Worcestershire sauce
15 ml/1 tbsp light soy sauce
15 ml/1 tbsp oyster sauce
15 ml/1 tbsp sugar
white pepper

*thin egg noodles*

*fresh root ginger*

*pork fillet*

*garlic*

*beansprouts*

*green and red peppers*

*light soy sauce*

**1** Boil the egg noodles according to the packet instructions and drain. Using a sharp chopping knife, carefully cut the pork fillet into 3–4-cm/1¼–1½-in strips and season with plenty of salt and pepper. Next, heat 7.5 ml/1½ tsp of the oil in a large frying pan or wok and stir-fry the pork until just cooked, then transfer to a dish.

**2** Wipe the pan with kitchen paper, and heat the remaining oil. Add the ginger, garlic and cabbage and stir-fry for 1 minute.

**3** Add the beansprouts and stir until softened, then add the green and red peppers and stir-fry for 1 minute.

**4** Return the pork to the pan and add the noodles. Stir in all the seasoning ingredients together with a little white pepper. Stir-fry for 2–3 minutes. Sprinkle with the ao-nori seaweed, if using.

# Indonesian Courgettes with Noodles

Any courgette or member of the squash family can be used in this quick and refreshing Indonesian dish, called *oseng oseng*.

*Serves 4–6*

INGREDIENTS
450 g/1 lb courgettes, sliced
1 onion, finely sliced
1 garlic clove, finely chopped
30 ml/2 tbsp sunflower oil
2.5 ml/½ tsp ground turmeric
2 tomatoes, chopped
45 ml/3 tbsp water
115 g/4 oz cooked, peeled prawns, (optional)
25 g/1 oz cellophane noodles
salt

*courgettes*

*ground turmeric*

*tomatoes*

*prawns*

*cellophane noodles*

*onion*

*garlic*

**1** Use a potato peeler to cut thin strips from the outside of each courgette. Cut them in neat slices. Set the courgettes on one side.

**2** Fry the onion and garlic in hot oil; do not allow them to brown. Add the turmeric, courgette slices, chopped tomatoes, water and prawns, if using.

**3** Put the noodles in a pan and pour over boiling water to cover, leave for a minute and then drain. Cut the noodles in 5 cm/2 in lengths and add to the vegetables.

**4** Cover with a lid and allow the noodles to cook in their own steam for 2–3 minutes. Gently toss everything well together. Season with salt to taste and serve while still hot.

## COOK'S TIP

Courgettes should be firm with a glossy, healthy looking skin. Avoid any that feel squashy or generally look limp, as they will be dry and not worth using.

# Gingered Chicken Noodles

A blend of ginger, spices and coconut milk flavours, this delicious supper dish is made in minutes. For a real oriental touch, add a little fish sauce to taste, just before serving.

## Serves 2–4

INGREDIENTS
350 g/12 oz boneless, skinless
    chicken breasts
225 g/8 oz courgettes
275 g/10 oz aubergine
about 30 ml/2 tbsp oil
5 cm/2 in fresh root ginger,
    finely chopped
6 spring onions, sliced
10 ml/2 tsp Thai green curry paste
400 ml/14 fl oz/1⅔ cups coconut
    milk
475 ml/16 fl oz/2 cups chicken stock
115 g/4 oz medium egg noodles
45 ml/3 tbsp chopped fresh
    coriander
15 ml/1 tbsp lemon juice
salt and white pepper
chopped fresh coriander, to garnish

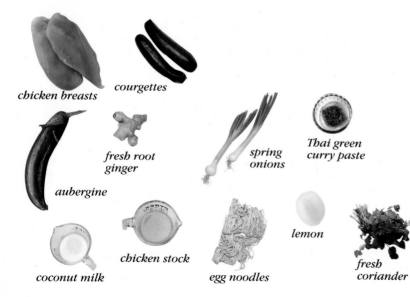

*chicken breasts*  *courgettes*

*fresh root ginger*  *spring onions*  *Thai green curry paste*

*aubergine*

*coconut milk*  *chicken stock*  *egg noodles*  *lemon*  *fresh coriander*

**1** Cut the chicken into bite-size pieces. Halve the courgettes lengthways and roughly chop them. Cut the aubergine into similarly sized pieces.

**2** Heat the oil in a large saucepan or wok and cook the chicken pieces, in batches if necessary, until golden. Remove the pieces with a slotted spoon and leave to drain on kitchen paper.

## COOK'S TIP
Very popular throughout South-east Asia, fish sauce can range in colour from ochre to deep brown. It is a pungent liquid that has a strong and salty flavour, so should only be used sparingly if unsure.

**3** Add a little more oil, if necessary, and cook the ginger and spring onions for 3 minutes. Add the courgettes and cook for 2–3 minutes. Stir in the curry paste and cook for 1 minute. Add the coconut milk, stock, aubergine and chicken, and simmer for 10 minutes.

**4** Add the noodles and cook for a further 5 minutes, or until the chicken is cooked and the noodles are tender. Stir in the chopped coriander and lemon juice and adjust the seasoning. Serve garnished with chopped coriander.

# Bamie Goreng

This fried noodle dish from Indonesia is wonderfully accommodating. To the basic recipe you can add other vegetables, such as mushrooms, tiny pieces of courgette, broccoli, leeks or beansprouts, if you prefer.

*Serves 6*

INGREDIENTS

450 g/1 lb dried egg noodles
1 boneless, skinless chicken breast
115 g/4 oz pork fillet
115 g/4 oz calves' liver (optional)
2 eggs, beaten
90 ml/6 tbsp oil
25 g/1 oz/2 tbsp butter
2 garlic cloves, crushed
115 g/4 oz cooked, peeled prawns
115 g/4 oz spinach or Chinese leaves
2 celery sticks, finely sliced
4 spring onions, cut into strips
about 60 ml/4 tbsp chicken stock
dark and light soy sauce
1 onion, thinly sliced
oil, for deep-frying
salt and freshly ground black pepper
celery leaves, to garnish

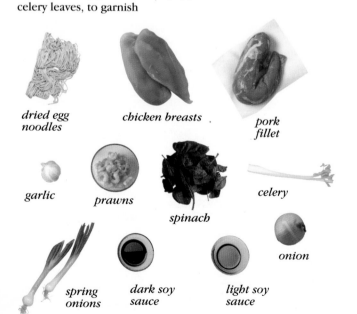

*dried egg noodles*
*chicken breasts*
*pork fillet*
*garlic*
*prawns*
*spinach*
*celery*
*onion*
*spring onions*
*dark soy sauce*
*light soy sauce*

**1** Cook the noodles in boiling, salted water for 3–4 minutes. Drain, rinse with cold water and drain again. Set aside until required.

**2** Using a small, sharp chopping knife, finely slice the chicken breast, pork fillet and calves' liver, if using.

**3** Season the eggs. Heat 5 ml/1 tsp of the oil with the butter in a small pan until melted and then stir in the eggs and keep stirring until scrambled. Set aside.

**4** Heat the remaining oil in a wok and fry the garlic with the chicken, pork and liver for 2–3 minutes. Add the prawns, spinach or Chinese leaves, celery and spring onions, tossing well. Add the noodles and toss well. Add enough stock to moisten the noodles and dark and light soy sauce to taste.

**5** In a separate wok or deep-fat fryer, deep-fry the onion until crisp and golden, turning constantly. Drain well. Stir the scrambled egg into the noodles and serve garnished with the deep-fried onion and celery leaves.

# Beef Noodles with Orange and Ginger

Stir-frying is one of the best ways to cook with the minimum of fat. It's also one of the quickest ways to cook, but you do need to choose tender meat.

*Serves 4*

INGREDIENTS

450 g/1 lb lean beef, e.g. rump, fillet or sirloin steak, cut into thin strips
finely grated rind and juice of 1 orange
15 ml/1 tbsp light soy sauce
5 ml/1 tsp cornflour
2.5 cm/1 in fresh root ginger, finely chopped
175 g/6 oz rice noodles
10 ml/2 tsp sesame oil
15 ml/1 tbsp sunflower oil
1 large carrot, cut into thin strips
2 spring onions, thinly sliced

*rump steak*

*orange*

*light soy sauce*

*fresh root ginger*

*carrot*

*sesame oil*

*spring onions*

*rice noodles*

**1** Place the beef in a bowl and sprinkle over the orange rind and juice. If possible, leave to marinate for at least 30 minutes.

**2** Drain the liquid from the meat and set aside, then mix the meat with the soy sauce, cornflour and ginger. Cook the noodles according to the instructions on the packet. Drain well, toss with the sesame oil and keep warm.

**3** Heat the sunflower oil in a wok or large frying pan and add the beef. Stir-fry for 1 minute until lightly coloured, then add the carrot and stir-fry for a further 2–3 minutes.

**4** Stir in the spring onions and the reserved liquid from the meat, then cook, stirring, until boiling and thickened. Serve hot with the rice noodles.

# Stir-fried Sweet-and-Sour Chicken

As well as quick, this South East Asian dish is decidedly tasty and you will find yourself making it again and again.

*Serves 3–4*

INGREDIENTS

275 g/10 oz dried medium egg
    noodles
30 ml/2 tbsp oil
3 spring onions, chopped
1 garlic clove, crushed
2.5 cm/1 in fresh root ginger, grated
5 ml/1 tsp paprika
5 ml/1 tsp ground coriander
3 boneless chicken breasts, sliced
225 g/8 oz sugar snap peas, topped
    and tailed
115 g/4 oz baby sweetcorn, halved
225 g/8 oz/1 cup beansprouts
15 ml/1 tbsp cornflour
45 ml/3 tbsp light soy sauce
45 ml/3 tbsp lemon juice
15 ml/1 tbsp sugar
45 ml/3 tbsp chopped fresh
    coriander, to garnish

*egg noodles*

*spring onions*

*garlic*

*ground coriander*

*chicken breasts*

*beansprouts*

*fresh coriander*

**1** Bring a large saucepan of salted water to the boil. Add the noodles and cook according to the packet instructions. Drain thoroughly, cover and keep warm.

**2** Heat the oil. Add the spring onions and cook over a gentle heat. Mix in the next five ingredients, then stir-fry for 3–4 minutes. Add the next three ingredients and cook briefly. Add the noodles.

**3** Combine the cornflour, soy sauce, lemon juice and sugar in a small bowl. Add to the wok and simmer briefly to thicken. Serve garnished with chopped fresh coriander.

## COOK'S TIP

Large wok lids are cumbersome and can be difficult to store in a small kitchen. Consider placing a circle of greaseproof paper against the food surface to keep cooking juices in.

# Cellophane Noodles with Pork

Cellophane noodles absorb liquid at four times their weight and have the ability of taking on the flavour of the ingredients they are cooked with.

## Serves 3–4

INGREDIENTS

115 g/4 oz cellophane noodles
4 dried Chinese black mushrooms
225 g/8 oz pork fillet
30 ml/2 tbsp dark soy sauce
30 ml/2 tbsp Chinese rice wine
2 garlic cloves, crushed
15 ml/1 tbsp grated fresh root
    ginger
5 ml/1 tsp chilli oil
45 ml/3 tbsp oil
4–6 spring onions, chopped
5 ml/1 tsp cornflour blended with
    175 ml/6 fl oz/¾ cup chicken
    stock or water
30 ml/2 tbsp chopped fresh
    coriander
salt and freshly ground black pepper
coriander sprigs, to garnish

*cellophane noodles*

*Chinese mushrooms*

*pork fillet*

*dark soy sauce*

*garlic*

*fresh coriander*

*spring onions*

*chicken stock*

*fresh root ginger*

**1** Put the noodles and mushrooms in separate bowls and cover them with warm water. Leave to soak for 15–20 minutes, until soft; drain well. Cut the noodles into 13-cm/5-in lengths. Squeeze any water from the mushrooms, discard the stems and finely chop the caps.

**2** Cut the pork into very small cubes. Put into a bowl with the soy sauce, rice wine, garlic, ginger and chilli oil, then leave for about 15 minutes. Drain, reserving the marinade.

**3** Heat the oil in a wok and add the pork and mushrooms. Stir-fry for 3 minutes. Add the spring onions and stir-fry for 1 minute. Stir in the chicken stock, marinade and seasoning.

**4** Add the noodles and stir-fry for about 2 minutes, until the noodles absorb most of the liquid and the pork is cooked through. Stir in the coriander. Serve garnished with coriander sprigs.

# Noodles with Ginger and Coriander

Here is a simple noodle dish that goes well with most oriental dishes. It can also be served as a snack for 2–3 people.

*Serves 4*

INGREDIENTS
handful of fresh coriander
225 g/8 oz dried egg noodles
45 ml/3 tbsp oil
5 cm/2 in fresh root ginger, cut into fine shreds
6–8 spring onions, cut into shreds
30 ml/2 tbsp light soy sauce
salt and freshly ground black pepper

*fresh coriander*

*dried egg noodles*

*fresh root ginger*

*spring onions*

*light soy sauce*

**1** Strip the leaves from the coriander stalks. Pile them on to a chopping board and coarsely chop them using a cleaver or large, sharp knife.

**2** Cook the noodles according to the packet instructions. Rinse under cold water, drain well and then toss in 15 ml/1 tbsp of the oil.

**3** Heat a wok until hot, add the remaining oil and swirl it around. Add the ginger and stir-fry for a few seconds, then add the noodles and spring onions. Stir-fry for 3–4 minutes, until hot.

**4** Sprinkle over the soy sauce, coriander and seasoning. Toss well and serve at once.

## COOK'S TIP

As with many Thai, Singapore or Malaysian dishes, for best results use groundnut oil. Alternatively fry vegetables in sunflower oil, but toss noodles in sesame oil.

# Lemon Grass Prawns on Crisp Noodle Cake

For an elegant meal, make four individual noodle cakes instead of one.

## Serves 4

### INGREDIENTS

300 g/11 oz thin egg noodles
60 ml/4 tbsp oil
500 g/1¼ lb medium raw king prawns, peeled and deveined
2.5 ml/½ tsp ground coriander
15 ml/1 tbsp ground turmeric
2 garlic cloves, finely chopped
2 slices fresh root ginger, finely chopped
2 lemon grass stalks, finely chopped
2 shallots, finely chopped
15 ml/1 tbsp tomato purée
250 ml/8 fl oz/1 cup coconut cream
15–30 ml/1–2 tbsp fresh lime juice
15–30 ml/1–2 tbsp fish sauce
4–6 kaffir lime leaves (optional)
1 cucumber, peeled, seeded and cut into 5-cm/2-in sticks
1 tomato, seeded and cut into strips
2 red chillies, seeded and finely sliced
salt and freshly ground black pepper
2 spring onions, cut into thin strips, and a few coriander sprigs, to garnish

ground coriander

ground turmeric

garlic

fresh root ginger

lemon grass

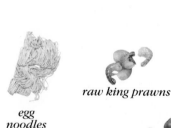
egg noodles

raw king prawns

shallots

tomato purée

coconut cream

kaffir lime leaves

fish sauce

cucumber

tomato

lime

red chillies

spring onions

fresh coriander

## COOK'S TIP
Coconut cream is available in cartons from supermarkets and oriental stores. It is richer than coconut milk, but this can be used if coconut cream is unavailable.

**1** Cook the egg noodles in a saucepan of boiling water until just tender. Drain, rinse under cold running water and drain well.

**2** Heat 15 ml/1 tbsp of the oil in a large frying pan. Add the noodles, distributing them evenly, and fry for 4–5 minutes, until crisp and golden. Turn the noodle cake over and fry the other side. Alternatively, make four individual cakes. Keep warm.

**3** In a bowl, toss the prawns with the ground coriander, turmeric, garlic, ginger and lemon grass. Season to taste. Heat the remaining oil in a frying pan. Add the shallots, fry for 1 minute, then add the prawns and fry for 2 minutes more before removing with a slotted spoon.

**4** Stir the tomato purée and coconut cream into the juices in the pan. Stir in lime juice to taste and season with the fish sauce. Bring the sauce to a simmer, return the prawns, then add the kaffir lime leaves, if using, and the cucumber. Simmer until the prawns are cooked.

**5** Add the tomato, stir until just warmed through, then add the chillies. Serve on top of the crisp noodle cake(s), garnished with strips of spring onions and coriander sprigs.

# Japanese Sweet Soy Salmon with Noodles

Teriyaki sauce forms the marinade for the salmon in this recipe. Served with soft-fried noodles, it makes a stunning dish.

## Serves 3–4

### INGREDIENTS

350 g/12 oz salmon fillet
30 ml/2 tbsp Japanese soy sauce (shoyu)
30 ml/2 tbsp sake
60 ml/4 tbsp mirin or sweet sherry
5 ml/1 tsp light brown soft sugar
10 ml/2 tsp grated fresh root ginger
3 garlic cloves, 1 crushed and 2 sliced into rounds
30 ml/2 tbsp groundnut oil
225 g/8 oz dried egg noodles, cooked and drained
50 g/2 oz alfalfa sprouts
30 ml/2 tbsp sesame seeds, lightly toasted

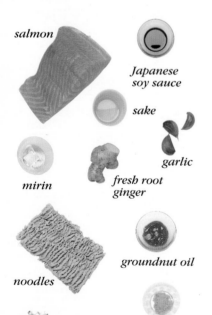

salmon

Japanese soy sauce

sake

garlic

mirin

fresh root ginger

groundnut oil

noodles

alfalfa sprouts

sesame seeds

**1** Using a sharp chopping knife, cut the salmon into thin slices, then place in a shallow dish.

**2** In a bowl, mix together the soy sauce, sake, mirin or sherry, sugar, ginger and crushed garlic. Pour over the salmon, cover and leave for 30 minutes.

**3** Preheat the grill. Drain the salmon, scraping off and reserving the marinade. Place the salmon in a single layer on a baking sheet. Cook under the grill for 2–3 minutes without turning.

**4** Meanwhile, heat a wok until hot, add the oil and swirl it around. Add the garlic rounds and cook until golden brown but not burnt.

**5** Add the cooked noodles and reserved marinade to the wok and stir-fry for 3–4 minutes, until the marinade has reduced slightly to a syrupy glaze and coats the noodles.

**6** Toss in the alfalfa sprouts, then remove immediately from the heat. Transfer to warmed serving plates and top with the salmon. Sprinkle with the toasted sesame seeds. Serve at once.

# Celebration Thai Noodles

This Thai speciality, called *mee krob*, is a crisp tangle of fried rice vermicelli tossed in a piquant sauce. It is served at weddings and other special occasions.

*Serves 4*

INGREDIENTS
oil, for deep-frying
175 g/6 oz rice vermicelli
15 ml/1 tbsp chopped garlic
4–6 dried chillies, seeded and chopped
30 ml/2 tbsp chopped shallot
15 ml/1 tbsp dried shrimps, rinsed
115 g/4 oz minced pork
115 g/4 oz uncooked, peeled prawns, chopped
30 ml/2 tbsp brown bean sauce
30 ml/2 tbsp rice wine vinegar
45 ml/3 tbsp fish sauce
75 g/3 tbsp palm sugar or soft brown sugar
30 ml/2 tbsp tamarind or lime juice
115 g/4 oz/½ cup beansprouts

FOR THE GARNISH
2 spring onions, cut into thin strips
fresh coriander leaves
2 heads pickled garlic (optional)
2-egg omelette, rolled and sliced
2 red chillies, seeded and chopped

*rice vermicelli noodles*  *garlic*  *chillies*

*dried shrimps*  *minced pork*  *uncooked prawns*

*beansprouts*  *spring onions*

**1** Heat the oil in a wok. Break the rice vermicelli apart into small handfuls about 7.5 cm/3 in long. Deep-fry in the hot oil until they puff up. Remove and drain on kitchen paper.

**2** Leave 30 ml/2 tbsp of the hot oil in the wok, add the garlic, chillies, shallots and dried shrimps. Fry until fragrant, then add the minced pork and stir-fry for about 3–4 minutes, until it is no longer pink. Add the prawns and fry for a further 2 minutes. Transfer the mixture to a plate and set aside.

**3** Stir the brown bean sauce, vinegar, fish sauce and palm or brown sugar into the wok. Bring to a gentle boil, stir to dissolve the sugar and cook until thick and syrupy. Add the tamarind or lime juice and adjust the seasoning. It should be sweet, sour and salty.

**4** Reduce the heat. Add the pork and prawn mixture and the beansprouts to the sauce, stir to mix and then add the rice noodles, tossing gently to coat them with the sauce. Transfer the noodles to a platter. Garnish with spring onions, fresh coriander leaves, omelette strips, red chillies and pickled garlic, if liked.

# King Prawn Thai Noodles

This delicately flavoured dish is considered one of the national dishes of Thailand, where it is known as *phat thai*.

*Serves 4–6*

INGREDIENTS

350 g/12 oz rice noodles
45 ml/3 tbsp oil
15 ml/1 tbsp chopped garlic
16 uncooked king prawns, peeled, tails left intact and deveined
2 eggs, lightly beaten
15 ml/1 tbsp dried shrimps, rinsed
30 ml/2 tbsp pickled mooli (white radish)
50 g/2 oz fried beancurd, cut into small slivers
2.5 ml/½ tsp dried chilli flakes
115 g/4 oz Chinese chives, cut into 5-cm/2-in lengths
225 g/8 oz/1 cup beansprouts
50 g/2 oz roasted peanuts, coarsely ground
5 ml/1 tsp sugar
15 ml/1 tbsp dark soy sauce
30 ml/2 tbsp fish sauce
30 ml/2 tbsp tamarind or lime juice
fresh coriander leaves, to garnish
lime wedges, to serve (optional)

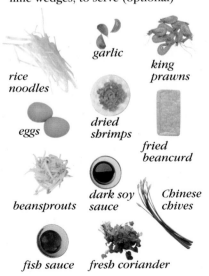

rice noodles

garlic

king prawns

eggs

dried shrimps

fried beancurd

beansprouts

dark soy sauce

Chinese chives

fish sauce

fresh coriander

**1** Soak the noodles in warm water for 20–30 minutes, then drain. Heat 15 ml/1 tbsp of the oil in a wok or large frying pan. Add the garlic and fry until golden. Stir in the prawns and cook for about 1–2 minutes, until pink, tossing from time to time. Transfer to a plate.

**2** Heat a further 15 ml/1 tbsp of oil in the wok. Add the eggs, tilting the wok to spread them into a thin sheet. Scramble and then transfer to a plate and set aside. Heat the remaining oil and add the dried shrimps, pickled mooli, beancurd and dried chilli flakes. Stir briefly.

**3** Add the noodles and stir-fry for 5 minutes, then add the Chinese chives, half the beansprouts and half the peanuts. Season with the sugar, soy sauce, fish sauce and tamarind or lime juice. Mix well.

**4** When the noodles are cooked through, return the prawns and cooked eggs to the wok and mix together. Serve garnished with the rest of the beansprouts, peanuts and the coriander leaves, with lime wedges if you wish.

# Beef and Vegetables in Table-top Broth

The perfect introduction to Japanese cooking, this dish is well suited to party gatherings.

*Serves 4–6*

### INGREDIENTS

450 g/1 lb sirloin beef, trimmed
1.75 litres/3 pints/7½ cups kombu and bonito stock or ½ sachet instant dashi powder, or ½ vegetable stock cube with 1.75 litres/3 pints/7½ cups water
150 g/5 oz carrots
6 spring onions, trimmed and sliced
150 g/5 oz Chinese leaves, roughly shredded
225 g/8 oz mooli (white radish), peeled and shredded
275 g/10 oz udon or fine wheat noodles, cooked
115 g/4 oz canned bamboo shoots, sliced
175 g/6 oz beancurd, cut into large dice
10 shiitake mushrooms

### FOR THE SESAME DIPPING SAUCE

50 g/2 oz sesame seeds or 30 ml/2 tbsp tahini paste
120 ml/4 fl oz/½ cup instant dashi stock or vegetable stock
60 ml/4 tbsp dark soy sauce
10 ml/2 tsp sugar
30 ml/2 tbsp sake (optional)
10 ml/2 tsp wasabi powder (optional)

### FOR THE PONZU DIPPING SAUCE

75 ml/5 tbsp lemon juice
15 ml/1 tbsp rice wine or white wine vinegar
75 ml/5 tbsp dark soy sauce
15 ml/1 tbsp tamari sauce
15 ml/1 tbsp mirin or 1 tsp sugar
1.5 ml/¼ tsp instant dashi powder or ¼ vegetable stock cube

*beef*

*kombu and bonito stock*

*carrots*

*spring onions*

*Chinese leaves*

*udon noodles*

*bamboo shoots*

*beancurd*

*shiitake mushrooms*

*sesame seeds*

*dark soy sauce*

*sake*

*lemon juice*

*mirin*

**1** Slice the meat thinly with a large knife or cleaver. Arrange neatly on a plate, cover and set aside. In a Japanese donabe, or any other covered, flameproof casserole that is unglazed on the outside, bring the kombu and bonito stock, dashi powder or stock cube and water to the boil. Cover and simmer for 8–10 minutes. Place at the table, standing on its own heat source.

**2** To prepare the vegetables, bring a saucepan of salted water to the boil. Peel the carrots and with a canelle knife cut a series of grooves along their length. Slice the carrots thinly and blanch for 2–3 minutes. Blanch the spring onions, Chinese leaves and mooli for the same time. Arrange the vegetables with the noodles, bamboo shoots and beancurd. Slice the mushrooms.

**3** To make the sesame dipping sauce, dry-fry the sesame seeds, if using, in a heavy frying pan, taking care not to burn them. Grind the seeds smoothly using a pestle and mortar with a rough surface. Alternatively, you can use tahini paste. Add the remaining sesame dipping sauce ingredients, combine well, then pour into a shallow dish.

**4** To make the ponzu dipping sauce, put the ingredients into a screw-top jar and shake well. Provide your guests with chopsticks and individual bowls, so they can help themselves to what they want. The idea is to cook their choice of meat and vegetables in the stock and flavour these with either the sesame or ponzu dipping sauces. Towards the end of the meal, each guest takes a portion of noodles and ladles the well-flavoured stock over them.

# Clay Pot of Chilli Squid and Noodles

This dish is delicious in its own right, or served as part of a larger Chinese meal, with other meat or fish dishes and rice.

*Serves 2–4*

INGREDIENTS

675 g/1½ lb fresh squid
30 ml/2 tbsp oil
3 slices fresh root ginger,
   finely chopped
2 garlic cloves, finely chopped
1 red onion, finely sliced
1 carrot, finely sliced
1 celery stick, sliced
   diagonally
50 g/2 oz sugar snap peas, topped
   and tailed
5 ml/1 tsp sugar
15 ml/1 tbsp chilli bean paste
2.5 ml/½ tsp chilli powder
75 g/3 oz cellophane noodles,
   soaked in hot water until soft
120 ml/4 fl oz/½ cup chicken stock
   or water
15 ml/1 tbsp light soy sauce
15 ml/1 tbsp oyster sauce
5 ml/1 tsp sesame oil
pinch of salt
fresh coriander leaves, to garnish

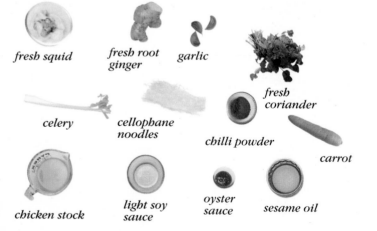

*fresh squid*   *fresh root ginger*   *garlic*

*celery*   *cellophane noodles*   *fresh coriander*

*chilli powder*

*carrot*

*chicken stock*   *light soy sauce*   *oyster sauce*   *sesame oil*

**1** Prepare the squid. Holding the body in one hand, gently pull away the head and tentacles. Discard the head; trim and reserve the tentacles. Remove the 'quill' from inside the body of the squid. Peel off the brown skin on the outside. Rub salt into the squid and wash under water. Cut the body of the squid into rings or split it open lengthways, score criss-cross patterns on the inside of the body and cut it into 5 x 4-cm/2 x 1½-in pieces.

**2** Heat the oil in a large, flameproof casserole or wok. Add the ginger, garlic and onion and fry for 1–2 minutes. Add the squid, carrot, celery and sugar snap peas. Fry until the squid curls up. Season with salt and sugar and then stir in the chilli bean paste and powder. Transfer the mixture to a bowl and set aside until required. Drain the soaked noodles and add to the casserole or wok.

**3** Stir in the chicken stock or water, light soy sauce and oyster sauce. Cover and cook over a medium heat for 10 minutes or until the noodles are tender. Return the squid and vegetable mixture to the pot.

**4** Cover and cook for a further 5–6 minutes, until all the flavours are combined. Season to taste.

**5** Spoon the mixture into a warmed clay pot and drizzle with the sesame oil. Sprinkle with the coriander leaves and serve immediately.

## COOK'S TIP

These noodles have a smooth, light texture that readily absorbs the other flavours in the dish. To vary the flavour, the vegetables can be altered according to what is available.

# Tiger Prawn and Lap Cheong Noodles

*Lap cheong* is a special air-dried Chinese sausage. It is available from most Chinese supermarkets. If you cannot buy it, replace with diced ham, chorizo or salami.

*Serves 4–6*

### INGREDIENTS
45 ml/3 tbsp oil
2 garlic cloves, sliced
5 ml/1 tsp chopped fresh root ginger
2 red chillies, seeded and chopped
2 lap cheong, about 75 g/3 oz, rinsed and sliced (optional)
1 boneless chicken breast, thinly sliced
16 uncooked tiger prawns, peeled, tails left intact and deveined
115 g/4 oz green beans
225 g/8 oz/1 cup beansprouts
50 g/2 oz Chinese chives
450 g/1 lb egg noodles, cooked in boiling water until tender
30 ml/2 tbsp dark soy sauce
15 ml/1 tbsp oyster sauce
salt and freshly ground black pepper
15 ml/1 tbsp sesame oil
2 spring onions, cut into strips, and fresh coriander leaves, to garnish

*red chillies*

*chicken breast*

*prawns*

*garlic*

*green beans*

*beansprouts*

*Chinese chives*

*egg noodles*

*dark soy sauce*

*fresh root ginger*

*oyster sauce*

*sesame oil*

*spring onions*

*coriander*

Chinese chives, sometimes called garlic chives, have a delicate garlic/onion flavour. If they are not available, use the green parts of spring onions.

**1** Heat 15 ml/1 tbsp of the oil in a wok or large frying pan and fry the garlic, ginger and chillies.

**2** Add the lap cheong, chicken, prawns and beans. Stir-fry for about 2 minutes over a high heat or until the chicken and prawns are cooked. Transfer the mixture to a bowl and set aside.

**3** Heat the remaining oil in the wok and add the beansprouts and Chinese chives. Stir-fry for 1–2 minutes.

**4** Add the noodles and toss and stir to mix. Season with soy sauce, oyster sauce, salt and pepper.

**5** Return the prawn mixture to the wok. Reheat and mix well with the noodles. Stir in the sesame oil. Serve garnished with spring onions and coriander leaves.

# Luxury Fried Noodles

This makes a tasty side dish for three to four people or a meal for two people, served with just a separate vegetable or meat dish.

## Serves 2–4

### INGREDIENTS

40 g/1½ oz dried Chinese
   mushrooms
275 g/10 oz fine egg noodles
15 ml/1 tbsp sesame oil
45 ml/3 tbsp oil
2 garlic cloves, crushed
1 onion, chopped
2 green chillies, seeded and thinly
   sliced
15 ml/1 tbsp curry powder
175 g/6 oz green beans
115 g/4 oz Chinese leaves, thinly
   shredded
6 spring onions, sliced
45 ml/3 tbsp dark soy sauce
175 g/6 oz cooked, peeled prawns
salt

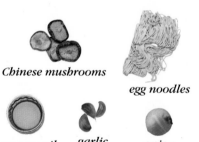

*Chinese mushrooms*

*egg noodles*

*sesame oil*   *garlic*   *onion*

*green chillies*   *curry powder*

*green beans*   *Chinese leaves*

*prawns*   *dark soy sauce*   *spring onions*

**1** Place the mushrooms in a bowl. Cover with warm water and soak for 30 minutes. Drain, reserving 45 ml/3 tbsp of the soaking water, then slice, discarding the stems.

**2** Cook the noodles in a pan of lightly salted boiling water according to the directions on the packet. Drain, place in a bowl and toss with the sesame oil.

**3** Heat a wok, add the oil and stir-fry the garlic, onion and chillies for 3 minutes. Stir in the curry powder and cook for 1 minute, then add the mushrooms, beans, Chinese leaves and spring oni full stop.

**4** Add the noodles, soy sauce, reserved mushroom soaking water and prawns. Toss over the heat for 2–3 minutes, until the noodles and prawns are heated through, then serve.

# Chicken Curry with Rice Vermicelli

**Lemon grass gives this South East Asian curry a wonderful, lemony flavour and fragrance.**

*Serves 4*

INGREDIENTS
1 chicken, about 1.5 kg/3–3½ lb
225 g/8 oz sweet potatoes
60 ml/4 tbsp oil
1 onion, finely sliced
3 garlic cloves, crushed
30–45 ml/2–3 tbsp Thai curry
    powder
5 ml/1 tsp sugar
10 ml/2 tsp fish sauce
600 ml/1 pint/2½ cups coconut milk
1 lemon grass stalk, cut in half
350 g/12 oz rice vermicelli, soaked
    in hot water until soft
salt

FOR THE GARNISH
115 g/4 oz/½ cup beansprouts
2 spring onions, finely sliced
    diagonally
2 red chillies, seeded and finely
    sliced
8–10 mint leaves

*chicken*

*Thai curry powder*

*coconut milk*

*rice vermicelli noodles*

*lemon grass*

*beansprouts*

*mint leaves*

*red chillies*

*spring onions*

**1** Skin the chicken. Cut the flesh into small pieces. Peel the sweet potatoes and cut them into large chunks, about the size of the chicken pieces.

**2** Heat half the oil in a large, heavy saucepan. Add the onion and garlic and fry until the onion softens. Add the chicken pieces and stir-fry until they change colour. Stir in the curry powder. Season with salt and sugar and mix thoroughly, then add the fish sauce, coconut milk and lemon grass. Cook over a low heat for 15 minutes.

**3** Meanwhile, heat the remaining oil in a large frying pan. Fry the sweet potatoes until lightly golden. Using a slotted spoon, add them to the chicken. Cook for 10–15 minutes more, or until both the chicken and sweet potatoes are tender.

**4** Drain the rice vermicelli and cook them in a saucepan of boiling water for 3–5 minutes. Drain well. Place in shallow bowls, with the chicken curry. Garnish with beansprouts, spring onions, chillies and mint leaves, and serve.

# Birthday Noodles with Hoisin Lamb

In China, the noodles served at birthday celebrations are left long: it is held that cutting them might shorten one's life.

*Serves 4*

INGREDIENTS
350 g/12 oz thick egg noodles
1 kg/2¼ lb lean neck fillets of lamb
30 ml/2 tbsp oil
115 g/4 oz fine green beans,
    blanched
salt and freshly ground black pepper
2 hard-boiled eggs, halved, and
    2 spring onions, finely shredded,
    to garnish

FOR THE MARINADE
2 garlic cloves, crushed
10 ml/2 tsp grated fresh root ginger
30 ml/2 tbsp dark soy sauce
30 ml/2 tbsp rice wine
1–2 dried red chillies
30 ml/2 tbsp oil

FOR THE SAUCE
15 ml/1 tbsp cornflour
30 ml/2 tbsp dark soy sauce
30 ml/2 tbsp rice wine
grated rind and juice of ½ orange
15 ml/1 tbsp hoisin sauce
15 ml/1 tbsp wine vinegar
5 ml/1 tsp soft, light brown sugar

*orange*   *green beans*   *lamb fillet*   *spring onions*   *garlic*

*fresh root ginger*   *dark soy sauce*   *hoisin sauce*   *eggs*   *wine vinegar*   *thick egg noodles*

**1** Bring a large saucepan of water to the boil. Add the noodles and cook for 2 minutes only. Drain, rinse under cold water and drain again. Set aside. Cut the lamb into 5-cm/2-in-thick medallions. Mix the ingredients for the marinade in a large, shallow dish. Add the lamb and leave to marinate for at least 4 hours or overnight.

**2** Heat the oil in a heavy-based saucepan or flameproof casserole. Fry the lamb for 5 minutes, until browned. Add just enough water to cover the meat. Bring to the boil, skim, then reduce the heat and simmer for 40 minutes or until the meat is tender, adding more water as necessary.

**3** Make the sauce. Blend the cornflour with the remaining ingredients in a bowl. Stir into the lamb and mix well without breaking up the meat.

**4** Add the noodles with the beans. Simmer gently until both the noodles and the beans are cooked. Add salt and pepper to taste. Divide the noodles among four large bowls, garnish each portion with half a hard-boiled egg, sprinkle with spring onions and serve.

# Chicken and Prawn Hot Pot

Using a portable hot pot, this dish, known as *Yosenabe*, combines meat, fish, vegetables and noodles to create a really warming meal that is cooked at the table.

*Serves 4*

INGREDIENTS
400 g/14 oz chicken thighs or breasts on the bone
8 uncooked tiger prawns
200 g/7 oz dried udon noodles
4 shiitake mushrooms, stems removed
½ bunch Chinese leaves, cut into 3-cm/1¼-in slices
3 leeks, sliced diagonally into pieces 1 cm/½ in-thick
15 x 10-cm/6 x 4-in piece beancurd (about 150 g/5 oz), cut into 3-cm/1¼-in cubes
300 g/11 oz shirataki noodles, boiled for 2 minutes, drained and halved

FOR THE YOSENABE STOCK
1 litre/1¾ pints/4 cups kombu and bonito stock
90 ml/6 tbsp sake or dry white wine
30 ml/2 tbsp dark soy sauce
20 ml/4 tsp mirin
10 ml/2 tsp salt

**1** Cut the chicken into 1-cm/½-in chunks. Remove the black intestinal vein from the prawns if necessary.

**2** Cook the udon noodles for 2 minutes less than the packet instructions, drain and rinse thoroughly, then drain again and set aside. Arrange all the remaining ingredients on large plates.

*chicken thighs*

*shiitake mushrooms*

*Chinese leaves*

*tiger prawns*

*leeks*

*udon noodles*

*sake*

*kombu and bonito stock*

*beancurd*

*mirin*

*dark soy sauce*

**3** Bring all the ingredients for the yosenabe stock to the boil in the hot pot. Add the chicken and simmer for 3 minutes, skimming the broth throughout cooking.

**4** Add the remaining ingredients, except the udon noodles and simmer for 5 minutes or until cooked. Diners serve themselves from the simmering hot pot. Finally, when all the ingredients have been eaten, add the udon noodles to the rest of the soup, heat through and serve in bowls to round off the meal.

# index